LEAD FROM NO

LEAD FROM NO

A SYSTEMATIC APPROACH
TO LEADERSHIP NEGOTIATION

JIM CAMP JR.

MANUSCRIPTS
PRESS

LEAD FROM NO
A Systematic Approach to Leadership Negotiation

ISBN 979-8-88926-171-1 *Paperback*
979-8-88926-172-8 *Hardcover*
979-8-88926-170-4 *Ebook*

To my grandkids,
who understand a "no" isn't the end of
an agreement but the start of an opportunity.

CONTENTS

INTRODUCTION

Reflecting on the events of September 11, 2001, the entire day is permanently ingrained in my memory. The somber feelings of unimaginable tragedy and loss, combined with witnessing our nation's heroic response, is unforgettable. Like many others, I'm sure, my experiences on this day led to a dramatic turning point in my career.

Back then I had three jobs. I flew for United Airlines, served part-time in the Air National Guard flying the KC-135 air refueler, and worked for my father's negotiation coaching business.

I knew sustaining all three would become unmanageable and decided to shift priorities. My immediate plans included separating from the military in October of 2001. I wanted to devote more time to my family and my father's business. On September 9, two days prior to 9/11, I flew the 767 out of Newark, where United Flight 93, the one where passengers fought back and crashed south of Pittsburgh, originated. After returning from my trip on the morning of 9/11, I headed to the 121st Air Refueling Wing in Columbus Ohio for a day of military flight training. I remember enjoying the weather with the top down in the Jeep. I first became aware of an aircraft crashing into the World Trade Center while listening to the radio. A routine day quickly turned into one filled with dread and concern.

Approaching the front gate of my base, I noticed more airmen than usual guarding the entrance. The heavily armed security team informed me the installation recently shifted to a real-world lockdown status. They checked my identification and let me know we were under a nationwide terrorism threat.

Walking into the flying squadron is normally a lot of fun. The camaraderie of the military and first responder community is unique. I miss all the teasing and bantering before flying. On this day, you could have heard a pin drop. All my teammates were staring at the TV in the corner of the room in disbelief. When another aircraft hit the second tower, we instantly knew this was a deliberate attack, and everyone in the room understood we were on the brink of war. Our state of shock turned into a sense of urgency after being directed to prepare for multiple response missions. We didn't have time to recall additional personnel, and those of us already in the flight room geared up for missions.

Our unit always had two tanker aircraft full of fuel, positioned and prepared to launch in a moment's notice. Although these aircraft were normally prepared to provide air refueling during a nuclear crisis, that day's mission, we responded to a threat our country hadn't experienced. When the details of the attack unfolded to include the strike on the Pentagon, my squadron commander ordered me and my crew to launch one of our alert aircraft. The entire squadron wanted to contribute to the response.

I quickly grabbed a copilot and a boom operator. Without the normal time to brief our mission or even file our flight plan, we hustled to launch and set up an air refueling orbit over the Pentagon. The normal preflight of the KC-135 required an hour. Within only twenty minutes, we pushed up the throttles for takeoff and headed to the east coast. The air traffic controller cleared us to fly any altitude, any airspeed, and gave us a direct route straight to Washington, DC. He also let us know the inbound international flights were diverted from their normal destinations and ordered to land all along the east coast and Canada. We were one of the only aircraft airborne east of the Mississippi River. Across the country, numerous jet fighters were also launching for the purpose of homeland defense. Given the events of the day, those fighter jets were ready to shoot down any rogue aircraft. Air Force One and the president were also on the move, and my crew and I assumed we'd refuel numerous fighters once we arrive.

From miles away we could see the dark smoke billowing up from the Pentagon. Processing the reality of this situation, my crew and I were speechless. Approaching our refueling location, the northeastern air defense sector came up on the radio and asked us to authenticate who we were and to verify we were on an authorized mission. This is a standard procedure during training, let alone in a crisis. Their airspace control callsign is Giant Killer. In the distance we could see the formation of F-16s rapidly approaching our jet. All at once, all three of us realized we had made a terrible mistake. This is the responsibility of the aircraft commander, and I instantly knew I blew it. In our rush to get off the ground, we didn't grab our communications secrets from the command post at Rickenbacker. Without our classified documents, we had no way of proving we were on an authorized response mission.

I had a pit in my stomach and a lump in my throat when Giant Killer asked us to authenticate by broadcasting "Charlie Mike." They expected a quick and proper response to their code words. We should have been able to open the classified response table and issue the correct reply. I can't forget the concerned look on my copilot's face. Normally, the pilot who is not flying the aircraft operates the radios. In this case, I took over the radios in addition to flying the jet. Giant Killer repeated their authentication request while the F-16s rolled in behind our aircraft. Hearing the increased stress in the controller's voice when he repeated his request, I remained calm and replied: "Giant Killer, this is Sluff 61, and I apologize. We have a problem. I didn't grab our communications kit before we launched. What can I do to assure you we are who we say we are?" A long period of uncomfortable silence followed.

The formation of four F-16s were divided with two on each side of our aircraft. This is a normal position before air refueling; however, this time they were a little closer than usual. They were also listening to Giant Killer and trying to get a closer look at our aircraft. From their point of view, the pilots could determine the base from which our aircraft originated. It seemed like a minute had gone by, and still no response from the controller. During Air Force pilot training, all pilots learn hand signals in case of radio silence or failure. When the F-16 flight lead got close enough, I made eye contact and popped a quick salute. I then used my left hand to show him the signal for refueling. No response. I'm sure they were uncomfortable during the moment, and they also needed our gas.

Still waiting for the controller to respond, I instructed our boom operator already in the back of our airplane to lower and extend the refueling boom. I again came up on voice and calmly said, "This is Captain Jim Camp. We launched out of the 121st Air Refueling Wing. We're unable to authenticate. My mistake. We have plenty of fuel to offload. We've completed our air refueling checklist. When would you like to take your gas?"

Thankfully, Giant Killer agreed and said, "You're cleared to conduct air refueling."

We were relieved when the fighters started taking our gas. Each aircraft connected one by one. While they were connected to our boom, we were able to have a short private conversation with the pilots. We could hear the stress in their voices. At this point, our crew is still unaware of the unraveling situation with Flight 93. A few hours later when we returned to base and conducted our mission debriefing, we humbly realized we could've been ordered to land—or worse.

Everything changed for my family and me after the morning of 9/11. I decided not to leave the military. With the support of my wife Cynthia and family, I volunteered to deploy, including the invasion of Iraq in 2003. While I stayed engaged with the family negotiation business, I took long-term military leave from United Airlines. The military became my primary focus. After resigning from the airline in 2006, I accepted a full-time military position as an instructor pilot. I planned to serve for another five years, retire militarily in 2010, then return to the world of negotiation. The family business continued to grow, and my father assured me I could come back anytime. I didn't anticipate how leading people would impact my life and career and didn't imagine serving until March of 2024.

In the military, when you reach tactical proficiency in your primary skill, which for me became instructing others how to fly the tanker, grooming for leadership positions becomes a bigger focus. Although I continued flying, my goal shifted to becoming a commander. To lead a flying squadron, being a good pilot isn't enough. Fortunately, my mentors encouraged me to take on challenging staff assignments, complete the requisite military education programs, and deploy in staff and leadership roles. Being selected for command is a competitive process, and it didn't come easy.

In retrospect, I'm thankful the journey to command is difficult. I heard "no" a few times before having the chance to lead my first squadron. Eventually I became a base commander and a commanding general of five thousand airmen. When I heard the word "no," instead of being discouraged, another door would open. "No" is only a decision and should not be considered a rejection or failure. A "no" is your opportunity to uncover what's behind the decision itself. I embraced the feedback from my peers and learned to control my intensity. I worked on my patience and listened to my mentors. Everything paid off.

During my journey to command, I discovered the strong connection between leadership and negotiation. Successful leaders negotiate daily. My military experiences reinforced why the word "no" is instrumental to our system of negotiation.

Recently transitioning out of the military and having conversations, my son James helped me rethink my contribution in the negotiation world.

In the spring of 2021, my family and I traveled to Boston. After graduating from the University of Chicago and serving six years on active duty in the United States Marine Corps commanding a sniper platoon, our son, James, graduated from MIT with his master of business administration. James was also enrolled in a master's program at the Harvard Kennedy School. During our visit, he happily showed us his grandfather's book, *Start with No*,[1] on the shelf in the Harvard bookstore. He also pointed out how the book was required reading for his negotiation class. Over a celebratory dinner with the family, we discussed leadership and his forthcoming transition into the private equity arena.

Based on James's experience in our country's finest academic institutions, and the outstanding leadership training in the Marines, we both agreed systematic negotiation training can help any leader. We also discussed my next steps and what it would look like for me to jump back into Camp Negotiations. During the visit, I shared with James and the family my intention to retire from the military. I planned to rejoin my brother, Todd, in the family business. James laughed and said, "This should be fun to watch. Maybe you should write a book someday." We'd frequently discussed my leadership journey, and he helped convince me to share my lessons learned. Over the years in command, James knew I negotiated constantly in all directions.

In 2002, my father and founder of our company, Jim Camp Sr., challenged the negotiation world and published *Start with No*. The lack of systematic negotiation coaching and training programs inspired my father to develop a system. Since then, our company, Camp Negotiations, has focused on a contrarian definition of negotiation: an agreement, or the effort to reach an agreement between two or more parties, with all parties having the right to veto. The critical component in this definition is the *right* of all parties to say no. You probably notice, the word "compromise" is not included in our definition.

If you believe negotiation requires compromise from both sides of the table, you're consistent with what most believe to be true. Words like win-win, give and take, collective bargaining, and protecting the relationship comes to mind when people think of the word "negotiation." Many of the programs and experts in the field also align to this notion. In fact, many teach the practice of determining a walk away point, or a pre-planned compromise.

Leadership training and coaching is also steered by preconceived notions. Most leadership training and coaching programs focus on leadership style, the characteristics of an effective leader, situational leadership methods, and how to develop good leaders.

You might be asking, "What do the two disciplines have in common?" Here it is: Although most higher-level academic institutions and countless authors, consultants, and training organizations are making significant contributions in both fields, I'm suggesting they interconnect.

The foundation for being an effective leader is your ability to negotiate strong agreements. Your first hurdle is embracing the word "no."

WHO SHOULD READ THIS BOOK AND WHY
This book is intended to help leaders at any level. Whether you're a CEO of a manufacturing company, an entrepreneur trying to build a business, a recent graduate

joining their first company, or a mid-level manager, I hope this book helps you.

Most view negotiation through the lens of sales, procurement, contracts, legal agreements, mergers, and acquisitions. The fact is, if you lead any number of people, you're continuously negotiating with members of your team. The trade-off for you taking the time to read this is that you'll discover leadership is the most frequent and important form of negotiation: a negotiation where your agreements are ongoing and fragile; an enduring deal where any person can walk away and leave your company or organization at any time. Whether you're negotiating peer-to-peer, working with subordinates, or leading up the chain, internal or external, agreements are everywhere and constantly in motion.

People on your team can say no at any time. Leaders not paying close attention to this learn the hard way. Your up-and-coming talent suddenly leaves the team, and everyone wonders what happened.

Let me be clear, leaders can always terminate agreements with teammates who don't produce or lack commitment. Both sides of the table have the right to say no. "No, I'm no longer going to work for this company." "No, I'm not acknowledged for my contributions." "No, I don't like the direction this organization is heading." "No, I don't have confidence in my leadership." Sadly, this happens due to poor leadership, or leaders who aren't connected with their players. We've all heard the saying, "People don't leave jobs, they leave bosses." A leader's job is to foster and sustain agreements with your team members. You want them to stay committed. No one, even in the military, is forced to stay. If they want out, they will find a way.

I consider negotiation and leadership human performance events. Your ability to perform well in either can improve by using a system, especially when it comes to managing your emotions. Look at the medical profession, aviation, the military, or sports like football: All are considered human performance events. Applying a systematic approach to these examples keeps everyone on the same path seeking a successful outcome. Without a game plan or process in place, keeping track of your progress can become too emotional and unmanageable. Systematic approaches are applied to many disciplines and professions, so why not negotiation and leadership?

Ways to improve our performance can include preparation, practice, training, coaching, and, of course, playing the game. Let's consider negotiation and leadership. Experts in both fields typically have a proven track record. If we ask how they became successful, or what their secret is to becoming a good leader, or how to become a good negotiator, can they produce a blueprint for success? Luckily, many experts write, lecture, and teach. This is a good thing. We've all benefited, including myself, from those paving the way in both disciplines. A challenge I see is most coaching programs are rooted in theories and derived from personal experiences. Although we're fortunate many have pioneered their principles and rules, my big question is, "Where's the systematic alignment?" Without a system, how does one diagnose a potential deal or solve a significant leadership challenge?

I'm personally thrilled business coaching has become popular. I've benefited from countless coaches and mentors. I hope by sharing my unique and combined experience in both fields, you'll begin to discover the connection and the advantage of adapting to a system. An easily understood system, thereby improving your emotional control.

From personal experience, leading an organization is complex, requiring countless skills and attributes. Although no one handed me a systematic guide to leadership (probably because one doesn't exist), I believe understanding the importance of the word "no" and our system of negotiation will help you establish tighter team alignment. I'm sure most leadership experts would agree when I say, strong followership is required for any organization to succeed. Followership implies agreements with leadership. Without forming strong agreements, your team's success is in jeopardy.

I also believe the strength of any organization is dependent on the cohesiveness of the team. Cohesion is improved when enduring agreements are negotiated at each level of leadership. Therefore, leadership is a critical form of negotiation.

Hopefully this book helps you see how negotiated agreements can impact your leadership success. By examining leadership and business scenarios, we'll focus on the mindset, structure, and behaviors supporting our system. I'll also help you embrace a person's right to say no. This alone will help you become more effective at reaching any agreement.

CHAPTER 1:

NEGOTIATION AND LEADERSHIP—A SYSTEM PROVIDES EMOTIONAL CONTROL

Changing behavior and adapting to a new system is difficult. Habits are hard to break, and learning a new approach to anything can be frustrating. I've seen many clients and fellow leaders get bogged down with emotions, especially with uncertainty and the fear of making mistakes.

From my experience in leadership and negotiation coaching, the key to gaining emotional control during a complex agreement is slowing down and applying a systematic approach. Using a sequential structure to understand the situation forces you to think pragmatically rather than becoming overwhelmed. Our coaches at Camp Negotiations have a saying: "Slow down in order to go fast." Decision making becomes quicker and more effective when you can step back and follow a proven process. In the introduction, I mentioned human performance. Following a trusted routine and system gives you an edge. Although I appreciated this during high school and college athletics, learning to fly in the military turned it up a notch.

When I started Air Force pilot training, visualizing myself earning wings in only one year seemed impossible. Like all other military specialties, training is thorough and systematic. The pace and expectations for students are grueling: twelve-hour days, long hours of study, and constantly being pushed to improve upon weaknesses.

Mornings in the flight room started with a daily training exercise my classmates and I dreaded. We called it "Stand Up." This intentionally nerve-wracking process gave all of us a knot in our stomach. You were instantly under the microscope in front of your teammates. An instructor would describe a challenging emergency then call on a random trainee to stand up and recite checklist procedures committed to memory. If the trainee stumbled mentally, panicked, or failed to initially handle the scenario in the correct way, they were removed from the flying schedule and given an unsatisfactory grade for the entire day of training. Any student with too many bad days in a row faced wash out.

The first steps during any emergency are the same, even today. What they teach today is fundamentally simple. First and foremost, maintain aircraft control. Second, analyze the situation. Third, take appropriate action. Don't crash the jet because you're consumed by a problem— keep flying. Determine what's going wrong, identify the correct checklist to execute, and make good decisions consistent with your training. Once the situation is properly addressed by running checklists, we were taught to remember three more things: aviate, navigate, and then communicate. Always in this order, don't deviate. Keep the aircraft safely flying, determine the direction to fly, and communicate your emergency to those ready to help. In other words, the flight is not over until you're walking away from the jet in one piece.

I experienced my first emergency with an engine fire in a T-37. I did everything by the book, except for the communication step. I forgot to let the control tower know I shut down one of my two engines. I safely landed the jet in the second month of training. How do you suppose they rewarded me? I earned a well-deserved "unsatisfactory" grade for the day. I remember thinking, due to the emotional trauma of an emergency, I'd get the afternoon off. Wrong. They made me repeat the entire training mission for failing to communicate my emergency.

By forcing us to approach each emergency systematically under pressure, and by committing critical procedures to memory, they helped us gain confidence. During the real thing, this is how we avoided panic.

The instructors knew the high likelihood of each student encountering malfunctions and emergencies. To reinforce the importance of the training, we often discussed previous training accidents, most of which were fatal. Most fatal training crashes were caused by students or instructors reacting too quickly and not following proper procedures. In addition to our morning routine of being put on the spot, we spent countless hours in the flight simulators. During each simulator event, my fellow students and I coped by joking how our instructors were trying to kill us. Not by giving us a problem too big to solve, they challenged our emotional control to stay within our system.

The only way a student would be cleared to take a multi-million-dollar jet solo is by proving their ability to fly safely and maintain emotional control. The rules and principles of our systematic training had to become second nature. Adapting to the military way of flying isn't easy, especially for those with too much civilian flight experience. Learning a new system is difficult, and old habits are hard to break.

To illustrate how a system provides emotional control, I'd like to share an extreme example I witnessed during a combat mission. In March of 2003, days after the start of the Iraq invasion, my crew and I found ourselves flying air refueling missions well inside the Iraqi border. During our pre-flight intelligence briefing, the commanders made the decision to send our tankers further north into the combat zone. Although the planning teams were concerned with anti-aircraft weapons still under the control of the Iraqi military, the command staff decided to take the risk of sending us deep into the combat zone and low to the ground.

In hindsight, we were better off not having defensive counter measures on the KC-135. This way we couldn't see what was shot in our direction. Our ground forces were advancing quickly from the south, necessitating close air support south of Baghdad. Our invasion game plan relied on those soldiers and Marines. When we arrived in our refueling orbit to refuel a formation of A-10 attack fighters, we were shocked at how quickly they requested gas.

The A-10 is an awesome aircraft for supporting ground forces. On this mission, they were loaded to the teeth with weapons. They burned more fuel than usual with their heavy payload. Literally minutes after the last jet completed refueling, we heard the call over the emergency radio frequency. One of the pilots we refueled took a direct hit in the tail section of his aircraft. His jet caught fire. Our crew listened intently to the emergency radio. The calmness in the pilot's voice impressed us. In a relaxed manner (due to his pilot training experiences, I'm sure), the pilot verbalized his situation. "I've taken a hit, my number one engine is on fire, and I'm running my checklist. I'm losing hydraulic pressure, and my flight controls are starting to get sluggish. The fire is out, but the oil pressure in my good engine is starting to fluctuate. I can see the Baghdad airport, and I'm headed there." A minute later he said, "I'm not going to make the runway. My altitude and air speed are within limits of my ejection seat. I'm getting out; I'm going to eject."

Those moments after he ejected were incredibly intense. We were frustrated not knowing the outcome for the young pilot. While the search and rescue efforts unfolded, we remained on location and refueled other aircraft participating in the recovery effort. Later in the evening and out of fuel, we climbed to a higher altitude and headed back to base. On the way back we heard the great news. The A-10 pilot had ejected safely. He floated down in his parachute and fortunately landed next to a group of our Marines.

Imagine being the pilot in that A-10. You're flying at night, you're getting shot at, your aircraft is on fire, you don't know if you'll live to tell your story, and you calmly say, "I'm getting out; I'm going to eject." How did he stay calm? I've asked myself the same question watching first responders or medical professionals in the ER.

The young pilot made an effective decision under severe duress, ultimately saving his life. After a medical evaluation and detailed debriefing of the situation, he flew on another mission only days after his ordeal. His systematic training paid off.

I know comparing the systematic training of a pilot to a leader improving in negotiation is a stretch. I'm suggesting a systematic approach to anything that provides you with more emotional control. A system is better than relying on past experiences and theory alone. If you're trying to grow personally or develop leaders within your organization, learning a proven system of negotiation produces lasting habit patterns.

Developing leaders is critical for any profession. The challenge facing the business world is retaining talent long enough to prepare younger executives for increasing responsibilities. In 2023, millennials were three times more likely to change jobs than any other generation. Although this has become more socially acceptable, many switch jobs in hopes of finding something bigger. Simply having a job is not enough. They want leadership inspiration in the workplace. Unfortunately, the cost of unsatisfied employees turning over is upward of thirty billion dollars a year.[1]

Bringing in an outsider with a fresh perspective can keep a team agile and effective. The question is, at what cost? Although an organization benefits from introducing new personnel into their culture, why are these talented folks on the move this often? More importantly, how effective has the leadership been convincing them to stay put? If young leaders are constantly transitioning, how do they gain the technical knowledge and organizational understanding to take on increased responsibilities?

This inclination to move from company to company too soon is costly. This can also derail the growth and continuity of your team. Adapting to a new position in the same company takes time; however, stepping into a totally new environment can take much longer.

In the military, many say it takes a year to learn a new job and understand the people, culture, and overall functionality of the organization. A young leader who changes jobs too often will not have the benefit of peaking in a position. The benefits of getting to know your people cannot be understated. The leader-follower bond takes time, and a lasting bond is developed over multiple agreements. How can a young leader establish trust and build relationships within a company if they always leave? The team working with a short-term leader will also suffer. They may not sense the need to follow them and could miss out on learning from a perceived "temporary" supervisor or manager.

In the military, new assignments and relocation are the norm. A good rule of thumb is to keep someone in a role long enough to make an impact. A common understanding in the service is: When you start to get comfortable in your current position, be ready to move on. Active-duty personnel and their families move in a two- to three-year cycle. This process is intentional to develop their leadership abilities. The military spends decades deliberately preparing people for high-level positions.

A military commander's job description includes identifying and developing the next commander. From my experience, a young leader doesn't need a promise of promotion or a guarantee for command in their future. What they really want is to reach a negotiated understanding of what's required for them to progress. They want to know where they stand and how to improve. In the absence of direct candid feedback from their boss, they will drift away and potentially leave the ranks altogether. I've provided feedback to many young leaders, and they don't always like hearing the truth. These conversations are tough for both sides. Approaching these hard negotiations using a system lowers the emotions on both sides of the table.

Whether you're currently supervising a small team or running a large company, part of your responsibility is to retain and grow your team. When employees are stagnant, underpaid, and unable see a path to advancement, they seek new opportunities. What's worse is when talent leaves simply because they don't have a connection with their leadership. Even if you have negative feedback for an employee, avoiding difficult conversations could give the impression you don't value their future. Maybe they'll agree to your suggested improvements. Maybe they were unaware of how you see their performance. The way you prepare for and approach these internal negotiations can mean the difference between losing talent or motivating a change in behavior.

The earlier a younger employee can learn how to negotiate, the better equipped they'll be in a leadership role. For example, let's imagine a young accountant's first job. After a few years of work experience and earning their CPA credential, without a clear track for advancement, they may look for another company. What agreements have been negotiated to provide a vision for their potential? Even if they only lead a handful of people on a modest accounting project, are they treated like a leader? Most importantly, how are they developing to handle the emotional challenges of leadership? Can they negotiate effectively within their small team? If they decide to stay with the company long term and grow into a CFO, I wonder how many negotiations they'll have over the span of their career. How many of these agreements will be internal versus external? From my experience, the internal ones happen sooner and are the most difficult to manage.

When an organization brings in talent from the outside, this can also pose a challenge. During a recent interview with Brigadier General Kenny Maynus, whom I served with for many years, we discussed the leadership challenges of stepping into a new environment. When I first met Kenny, he was a lieutenant colonel in the Air National Guard. He agreed to join my team in Mansfield, Ohio, in 2016. He'd spent most of his career serving in the state of West Virginia. Since his arrival in Ohio, he's held five positions and is currently the chief of staff for the Air National Guard.

His success and quick accession to his current rank is unprecedented. When I asked him how he managed to connect with his team in each assignment, he replied: "It's not the big me, little you… It's about understanding the team and everyone's roles and responsibilities. It's not about me, it's all about helping everyone feel respected and valued for their contribution to the overall mission. Getting everyone to agree to move in the same direction is not easy. It takes time and patience."

Witnessing his leadership in action, Kenny impressed me with his calm and rational style. He had a way of bringing a team together by quietly observing and simply asking questions. When I asked how he approached connecting with a new team, he replied, "There's no such thing as a checklist or how-to manual. You're on your own. You must pull from your own experiences working with both good and bad leaders. This took years, but eventually I was able to assemble tools in my toolbox."

He continued by saying, "You can't expect to reach people in a large group setting. You must capitalize on the individual conversations. Most importantly, you have to keep your emotions under control at all times. The younger leaders on your team are always watching how you handle yourself; emotions will interfere with a leader's purpose." Like many others successful leaders, Kenny did not have, or imagined, using a system of negotiation. When I shared with him the basics of our system and asked if this would have helped him earlier on in his career, he laughed and said, "Now I understand how you've been operating all these years. Absolutely."

Negotiations with talented employees don't happen soon, or often, enough. First-line leaders are not necessarily equipped to handle small internal negotiations. You might argue navigating through these hard situations is a necessary path to leadership. I agree, struggling leads to valuable experiences. I simply question if companies can do a better job cultivating first line leaders.

If this sounds familiar, you can begin by providing young leaders with a system helping them address typical leadership challenges. Help them answer the following:

- What do I do when I encounter a problem with my team?
- How do I break bad news?
- How do I get my team to go above and beyond the expectations laid out in their job description?
- How can I get them to see the big picture?

Communication skills are critical for all leaders, and effective negotiators are great communicators. Leading and negotiating are one and the same.

Over the course of any career, most jobs lead to increasing leadership responsibilities. Mine certainly did. For the young accountant, crunching numbers, building spreadsheets, managing a small team, then analyzing a potential merger can result in becoming a CFO. Regardless of the career, leadership brings with it increased accountability. More responsibilities drive the need for emotional control.

A CEO, company resident, or even an Air Force wing commander can find themselves getting pulled in many directions. Problems always pop up requiring your attention. When they do, you might have to negotiate a solution. Along with taking care of more people and handling a broader scope of issues, the ability to make agreements becomes more critical. I've found the internal ones keeping your team aligned are the most challenging.

My younger brother, Todd, would agree: The internal deals are the hardest. Over the past twenty-plus years, I've enjoyed watching him grow into a true expert in the field of negotiation. He took charge of Camp Negotiations after our father passed away in 2014. His ability to coach high-level, complex negotiations with such focus and passion is remarkable. He's been engaged in multiple industries. This year alone, he informed me there's over one billion dollars in play. After he had the pleasure of meeting Derek Blazensky, who at the time transitioned from venture capital, they have been coaching numerous venture-backed start-ups.

During an interview with Todd, I asked him what a systematic approach to negotiation provided to his clients. Here's his response:

> A system gives people a process, a method that eventually changes their mindset. My clients began shifting away from win-win and compromise. They simply didn't know any better. They couldn't conceptualize what a system would provide prior to working together. The inherent stress of that all or nothing world is unmatched. Not just for the investors taking a shot on

something really big, but in particular the leaders within the start-up. They're truly all-in.

Given turmoil in the Silicon Valley banking structure, and the rising interest rates of 2023, finding sources of funding is tough. These CEOs not only answer to their own internal teams, but they also have to answer to banks regarding large amounts of debt, institutional investors, and in many cases long lists of angel investors, which often include family and friends, all expecting results. Worrying about hitting next month's payroll, let alone completing an acquisition, is a pressure that's enough to cloud anyone's judgement.

They're getting ready to run out of money right when a larger company, who seems to have all the power and leverage, approaches them. They're almost always thinly capitalized and months away from having to make the dreaded decision to wind down the company. In addition to running out of cash, these entrepreneurs have to find a way to preserve their emotional fortitude required to press on. Having the stamina to ride it out becomes a factor. Everything's at stake. Even their personal lives are often at risk to taking large setbacks after years of fighting the good fight.

The higher the emotion, the more difficult effective decision making becomes. This is true for all decisions. Day in and day out, during each step in their potential deals, Todd and his partner, Derek, are helping the teams prepare for each iteration. After the call or meeting, he coaches them during the debrief. He shared more of his experience by saying:

> The process of these leaders systematically preparing for every critical agenda and debriefing after the fact keeps their emotions in check. These folks are having very difficult conversations with their board, with their investors, and especially with their own teams. This takes a lot of courage, and it's great to see their confidence go up dramatically after they rely on their new system at every turn.
>
> They see unexpected outcomes and positive results no matter how difficult the environment. You can actually see our young entrepreneurs develop as leaders right in front of you. They found a process they can rely on to help reduce the emotion for their entire team. Their team responds well, and they all seem to align with each other when it comes time to make some of the hardest decisions.

The emotional strain of leading any organization can be overwhelming, especially if you're a new boss. Leadership stress includes wondering how your team will receive you. Before accepting command of the 179th Airlift Wing in Mansfield, Ohio, in 2016, Brigadier General Todd Audet approached me minutes before the change of command ceremony, a ceremony where I accepted command following an incredible, well-liked leader. The general jokingly said

I looked nervous. I told him the truth and said, "Yes, of course. I'm getting ready to meet eleven hundred airmen."

He smirked and replied, "If I were you, I'd be terrified." He followed his humor with sincerity and said, "Relax, Jim. Speak from the heart and take care of your people. It's that easy. People will follow you. Just be yourself." The general didn't suggest the job would be easy. He knew it would be the challenge of a lifetime.

One thing's for certain: The people you lead in stressful times will mirror your behavior. If the leader's emotions aren't always under control, the organization will suffer. Obviously, a calm and focused demeanor is more effective than being reactive and erratic.

In addition to controlling emotion and forming alignment, a system will speed up to make hard decisions. The difficult conversations will be better received, and problems will be dealt with quickly.

In most of the coming chapters, we'll progress further into our negotiation system. You'll find the structure of preparation and debriefing short and practical. Easily committed to memory, my hope is you'll discover this can be done with little effort. All you'll need is a piece of paper.

CHAPTER 2

NEGOTIATION AND LEADERSHIP MINDSET

Two things predict negotiation and leadership success: your willingness to challenge the notion of compromise, and getting over the fear of the word "no." Both require a growth mindset.

Through years of coaching negotiation, the first step when working with new clients is to find out how they view the word "negotiation." With each client, we hear the conventional buzz words like "give and take," "win-win," "compromise," and "preserving the relationship."

Over the course of my military career, especially working with leaders, I've done something similar. I want to understand their leadership mindset by asking, "What makes a good leader?" You can imagine the range of answers to this question. After listening to their responses, I share my view: "Leading is more than your position, title, rank, or authority. I believe the foundation of being a good leader is the ability to reach agreements with your team."

Striking a lasting business agreement can be hard, especially when you have a fixed mindset where you're prone to early compromise. When the negotiator hears things like, "You better lower your price, or we need to meet in the middle," they may be prone to give in too early. Even if the deal is still acceptable to both sides, the habit of caving under pressure can mean leaving money on the table.

When the young leader senses dissent within their team, how do they react? Do they seek to understand why their team is pushing back, or do they simply rely on their position of authority? Which sounds easier? Unfortunately, taking the path of least resistance or simply relying on past experiences doesn't lead to growth.

The biggest challenge in negotiation coaching or mentoring a leader is helping them recognize the need to face their fears. In most cases, people fear the word "no." They associate the word with a failed deal or rejection by their team.

Most people are weighed down with the *need* to hear yes. The word means acceptance, winning, being in charge, or getting promoted. If you "need" anything as a negotiator or as a leader, it will hold you back from success.

According to Dr. Carol Dweck, two types of mindsets exist: fixed and growth. People who believe they can develop their intelligence and abilities over time have a growth mindset. Those who see their intelligence as static have a fixed mindset. This implies they may try to look smart and avoid appearing wrong.[1] Leaders who are unable to face their own shortcomings will always struggle to accept the idea of being told no by their followers. Without humility and the willingness to improve, growth is out of their reach for any leader.

IF YOU FEAR THE WORD "NO," GROWTH IS DIFFICULT

In 2012, at the rank of lieutenant colonel, I had a strong desire to elevate my service. I wanted to become a commander. After being told no to a squadron command position at my home unit in Ohio, I applied for a one-year tour in the 745th special operations squadron at Hurlburt Field in Florida. They flew a reconnaissance aircraft in Iraq and Afghanistan supporting special forces. The unit had highly experienced volunteer aviators and a well-established reputation.

Unable to connect with their commander, I made a point to fly down to Florida unannounced. I simply walked up to the squadron and knocked on the door. This didn't please the commander. Luckily, I convinced him to let me in. After an on-the-spot interview with a few other pilots, they welcomed me to the team. My permanent unit in Ohio liked the idea and agreed to hold my full-time position until I completed my one-year active-duty tour.

After joining the team and qualifying in the RC-26, I deployed with the squadron to a base in northern

Afghanistan in the spring of 2012. Prior to deploying with the new unit, the squadron commander asked if I wanted to stay behind and be his second in command. I declined his offer. Most of the highly experienced people in my new squadron had already deployed numerous times. I knew experiencing the mission and establishing credibility with the team would be wise before jumping into any leadership position.

Thirty days into my sixty-day deployment, I noticed low morale developing within our group. The Air Force announced the RC-26 would be divested, and the 745th special operations squadron would be decommissioned at the end of the year. Our deployed team took this news badly. The stress on the team from daily combat missions and uncertainty of the unit's future took a visible toll on our people. Coincidently, when the Air Force made this news official, the commander back home stepped down unexpectedly. On top of everything else, the unit's leadership team was suddenly falling apart.

In a conversation with my teammates over dinner, one of the pilots suggested I would be a perfect person to lead the unit. My outside perspective would be valuable leading the squadron through such a difficult transition. The outgoing commander back at the 745th in Florida supported the idea. Unlike my fellow teammates, I had a secure job waiting for me. I also knew my home unit in Ohio would be supportive if I stepped up and accepted a command assignment. Why not? I had the qualifications for my first command. Although I did not "need" this job, I certainly wanted the opportunity. This seemed like a difficult challenge, and I didn't fear rejection.

The next day I picked up the phone and called the colonel in charge back in Hurlburt, Florida, the headquarters of Air Force Special Operations Command. He acted surprised when I asked to command the unit. This isn't a typical way the Air Force selects a commander. With a sarcastic tone in his voice, he asked a simple question: "Do you even know who you'll be working for?"

I'm sure he didn't expect my reply: "Yes, sir, I'll work for the men and women serving in the 745th. I'll execute your intent and follow your orders; however, I'll work for these folks."

He said, "This isn't the response I expected, but I like your answer. You're hired. I'll meet you at the aircraft when you get back at the end of the month."

In taking this bold step, I had nothing to lose. He could have told me no. Similar to what we teach our negotiation clients, you *want* the deal, you don't *need* the deal. I knew deep down in my gut I could lead this incredible team of people who were facing extreme uncertainty.

This moment defined the development of my leadership mindset. I've since made it a habit to ask all leaders under my command: Who do you work for? Most answer by describing the leadership structure above them, which is normal. Of course, we all report to someone. We all have responsibilities and are held accountable for the teams we lead. However, I try to help them see a leader's primary purpose is helping their teammates succeed. You work for your team.

Reflecting on this year in command, I can say the challenges pushed me to my limits. I found myself negotiating with most members of the squadron. They all had to agree to focus on completing our mission in Afghanistan. They also needed to prepare themselves for finding another job when the squadron deactivated and shut down completely. Although conversations were difficult, the uncertainty everyone shared became the glue for holding the team together.

The sooner young leaders can develop their ability to negotiate effectively, the more they'll contribute to the overall culture of their organization. The leader sets the tone during adversity. We were a tight group. More than a decade later, everyone's career accomplishments are impressive. The adversity helped all of those serving in the 745th develop a growth mindset.

I imagine everyone reading this book already has a perception, or fixed mindset, on negotiation and leadership. This is normal. Take a moment of pause here and ask yourself these two questions:

1. How would you define negotiation?
2. How would you define leadership?

Did you envision results like signing the big deal and getting promoted to the corner office, or did you see yourself influencing a team to help them overcome adversity? A fixed mindset might change over time depending on results or circumstances. However, developing a growth mindset is a conscious decision. In our system of negotiation, a growth mindset is required. You cannot become fixated on results. You cannot manage results. We'll discuss more on this subject later in the book.

Similar to how my father's book, *Start with No*, challenged the conventional wisdom of "win-win" negotiation,[2] hopefully this book tests your current mindset. I doubt many professionals out there view leadership as the most popular and important form of negotiation. One might ask: Why is leadership negotiation important? If all forms of negotiation require effort from both sides, why expend extra effort when I can simply direct someone to fall in line? From my experience in the military, there's a difference between compliance and reaching an agreement. Yes, giving orders in a timely manner can be required. When time permits, however, help your team discover "why" your direction makes sense.

If you lead people, your ideas and direction will be better received by first creating a shared vision. Unfortunately, you can't *force* your team to share the same vision. Helping them discover how they, and the organization, benefit from your solution brings you closer to an agreement.

Leaders are expected to make timely decisions, and occasionally those might be autonomous. Although decisiveness is a good quality, if you have the time, spreading the decision and generating input from your team can build consensus and improve trust. In other words, be careful using position or authority to force your followers into an agreement. Leaders making decisions alone run the risk of damaging their internal relationships. A follower may not be inclined to reach an agreement if the leader's not willing to invite a discussion. Be careful of pushing too hard to sell your ideas.

To many, the word "sales" implies presenting your case, applying pressure, closing the deal, and convincing others to act. I would argue no one likes being "sold" anything. How do you react when a person lays on a heavy sales pitch with all the great reasons why you should buy their product? They may have good reasons for excitement over their product. However, the pressure you're experiencing makes it difficult to decide. Influential leaders and successful negotiators help people make decisions to solve problems. The moment you try to convince the other side, you show your need for their buy-in. This insecurity of needing to convince people can degrade trust unless you're willing to give others the right to say no.

When it comes to mindset in negotiation and leadership, the word "need" is dangerous. At the negotiation table, neediness will send the wrong signal to the other side. A good example is when a leader constantly demands respect. Earning respect and needing respect are two different things. We've all seen leaders needing credit for having all the answers. This is also a good way to appear needy.

Over the course of my military career, I've learned the power of putting your teammates by your side. Allow them to contribute when you're making a hard decision. With many diverse backgrounds and perspectives, having others address real challenges yields better solutions. Leaders set the tone, and not having all the answers is a great way to build cohesion. The most effective teams work together to determine what's right versus focusing on who's right. Mutually generated solutions lead to tighter agreements.

From 2020 until 2023 I had the pleasure of serving with our state command chief, Chief Master Sergeant Heidi Bunker. Heidi and I functioned like equals even though I commanded the team. Having numerous bases and over five thousand people to take care of is a demanding job. I discovered when your scope of leadership responsibility grows, you must surround yourself with people who will tell you what you have to hear, which is not always what you want to hear. Heidi filled this role. She didn't hold back from telling me no, because I welcomed her perspective. I'm forever grateful for her candor, support, and friendship.

Heidi is retired from the military and is a practicing licensed clinical counselor. When we recently spoke, she shared the following:

Bringing a team together to reach an agreement is a journey and a process in order to get it right. When you see your team as a resource, and you're willing to show humility by admitting you don't always have the answer, it builds trust. You send a signal of being a secure leader. By engaging people from the ground level, you're able to gather the information needed to make good decisions. A leader who is willing to spend time, in the flesh, in an open forum is meaningful to people, and it creates a connection.

THE IMPORTANCE OF STARTING WITH NO

While recently preparing for a negotiation coaching workshop with a private equity group, our coaching team conducted a survey to uncover the negotiation mindset of over fifty executives. What we discovered leading up to coaching was typical of other clients. Looking closely at how the team defined the word "negotiation," unless they'd already read *Start with No*, many responses indicated a compromise-based mindset. On our first virtual call leading up to the workshop, we discussed their survey results and presented our definition of negotiation.

The definition of negotiation, and focus on compromise, is always the starting point of our training and coaching. We're not suggesting compromise doesn't happen. Of course it does. Bargaining can be an effective business decision. This team challenged us. We wanted to help them avoid unnecessary compromise. If their leadership in all ten companies already has a compromise-based mindset, chances are the habit had already permeated through the entire organization.

Leading up to our large group workshop in the fall, we were happy to provide coaching help to one of their top executives. He recently submitted a written proposal to purchase a small startup, and a month passed by without a reply to his offer. When our client finally received feedback, it appeared his offer insulted one of the start-up owners. The first thing our client mentioned was preparing another offer. He wanted to prepare a compromise.

Line by line, they were internally strategizing on what they could give up in hopes of reaching a deal. The concessions our client wanted to offer the start-up were significant. He hoped the compromises would appear fair and preserve their relationship.

Although the start-up expressed displeasure with the previous terms, they still had not formally rejected our client's offer. Running out of cash and lacking the vendor relationships to scale their sales, the start-up's future looked questionable.

When we asked why he wanted to give concessions, he expressed the importance of this acquisition to the future of his company. Securing the rights of the technology and absorbing their list of clients offered a big upside. Simply put, he *needed* this deal.

Suggesting he give them the chance to formally reject the written offer on behalf of their employees, board, and investors, our client told us he didn't want to risk it. He said, "What if they walk away?" Fortunately, he followed our coaching guidance and held off putting compromises in another offer.

A few weeks later, after taking our advice, the start-up responded to his request asking for a decision and formally rejected the original offer. The negotiation continued, and our client uncovered the issues blocking the deal.

After more time had passed, and with worsening financial conditions, our client avoided early compromise when the start-up agreed to the original purchase terms without any changes in price. His team missed something in previous negotiations: a small detail regarding the integration of the start-up's key employees into the new structure of ownership.

We also discovered they were not insulted by the first offer. One owner over-inflated his perceived valuation and sent a scathing email without consulting his partners and board. This bluff from one owner could have triggered an unnecessary compromise. Allowing the start-up to formally reject their first offer perpetuated the negotiation. The deal was still in progress.

Our coaching team's priority for the big workshop was helping the private equity group change their mindset. If we were successful, their team would embrace our system, form internal alignment, and realize compromise isn't always required. They already saw how getting a "no" could unlock the real issues.

Why do we fear the word "no"? Why is this prevalent in today's business world? I believe our culture associates it with failure and rejection. "I didn't get the job," "I got cut from the team," or in my case, "I was rejected by all the schools in the Ivy League."

We've all told the salesperson, "Maybe; give me time to think it over." In fact, many of our negotiation coaching clients reach out to us when a deal gets stagnant, or the other side is fading away. Think of a time in your career when you heard the word "no." Did you give up? Or did you keep negotiating?

When Carnegie Mellon told me after my sophomore year to take a year off due to poor academic performance, I guess you could say they told me no. Instead of accepting those terms, and with the guidance from my dad, I elevated the negotiation to the president of the university. After numerous calls to his office, and although he declined to speak with me personally, he delegated the decision to the dean of student affairs. I asked the dean, "What can I do to prove to you I don't need a year off to get my act together?" Consequentially, we reached an agreement. I could come back at the end of the summer under one condition. If I didn't achieve a 3.0 GPA in the next semester, I'd face permanent expulsion. With my back against the wall, I took the deal.

With mounting student loans and no idea what I would do after graduation, I had to buckle down. Halfway through the football season, I made a hard decision and quit the team. Between practice and traveling for games, I couldn't keep up academically. Playing football and being a quarterback was a huge part of my life. Growing up in a football household with a family full of quarterbacks, what would my dad and family think? I won't forget his words: "Sounds like a good decision, Jim. You've probably learned everything you will from football. I'm proud of you." In the following spring, after getting the grades required to stay in school, I started working between classes to afford flying lessons. I wanted to fly jets in the military. I graduated on time and probably wouldn't be writing this today if I accepted the first "no" kicking me out of school.

If you lead people who negotiate on behalf of your organization, you must align them to a mindset which avoids unnecessary compromise.

We coach our clients to stay focused in their opponent's world. We train our clients to always remain respectful and honest, and we don't believe in tricks or tactics. We also don't subscribe to power and leverage. In leadership, power is a dangerous perception. Instead, demonstrating sincerity and transparency are more important.

To get more of what you want from any deal, you must embrace the right of your opponent to reject your solution. If you have a growth mindset, you'll begin to see how this impacts your success. If you want your team to align and agree to follow you, stop selling and start listening. While we transition to building vision, and how vision impacts decision making, this should become clear.

CHAPTER 3

DECISION MAKING— DON'T FEAR THE "NO"

Imagine you're sitting across from a potential client ready to start a sales negotiation. A company you've been pursuing finally agreed to take your meeting after numerous calls and email exchanges. You've prepared with your team, and your presentation is good to go. The data supporting your product is solid, and you're excited. After they hear your presentation, you're confident you'll earn their business. This could be huge for you and your company.

Now imagine yourself getting ready to address an entire military base, and you're delivering bad news. Even though the decision impacting your team isn't one you've made personally, you want to relay the message from higher headquarters. Despite the unit's decades of strong performance, including many combat deployments, their ramp full of aircraft will soon be empty forever. Their flying mission is changing to something completely unknown, cyberspace. This will not be easy. You're compelled to deliver this in person because you're the boss. The team will be crushed, and you have a knot in your stomach.

Would you consider the second scenario, talking to a military base, a negotiation? Would you prepare for both in the same way?

In both cases, you're trying to reach an agreement where all parties have the right to say no. Whether you're negotiating with a company interested in buying your product or trying to convince a large group of airmen to accept the challenge of changing missions, you're negotiating.

If a business-to-business (B2B) sale can take months requiring multiple decisions before you even get to the table, imagine telling your military team everything is going to change. How many collective decisions will they have to make? Will they keep the uniform on and continue to serve?

In either case, controlling your emotions is important. You can't afford to appear excited, nor can you come across frustrated or upset. How can you avoid becoming consumed with your desired results in either scenario? If you prepare for a "no" in both cases, you won't be surprised when you hear it. I'm not suggesting a pessimistic attitude. Be aware, your expectations and assumptions can affect your game plan and personal behavior. During any negotiation, you must focus on your opponent's world and not your own.

Can your emotions impact a potential sales customer or your military teammate's ability to make good decisions?

I've personally participated in and coached players in both examples. From my experience, the internal leadership negotiation with your team is far more challenging. Being tightly connected with your people leads to more emotion. The stronger the emotion, the more difficult decision-making becomes.

I know it might be hard for you to relate to the emotions surrounding a change of mission in the military. Maybe your experience of career changes is a better analogy. Imagine you have a choice. You can stay with your current company and see what happens or get ahead of the change and uproot your family. Here's a deeper background into my situation to provide more context.

DELIVERING BAD NEWS AND UNDERSTANDING HOW EMOTIONS IMPACT DECISIONS

Currently the Air Force is in the process of trading capacity for capability. After decades of fighting the global war on terror, staying relevant requires change. Numerous units across the country will need to modernize their equipment or face becoming obsolete. The nature of conflict is changing, and our competitors, like China, are becoming more capable at an accelerated pace. The recent creation of the Space Force is a perfect example of shifting priorities to align with the constantly evolving National Defense Strategy.

The Air Force recently selected my former unit, the 179th Airlift Wing in Mansfield, Ohio, for a new mission. The unit's history is impressive, and the town's economy is heavily dependent on the future of the base. The unit is also well known for being at the top of the national list for recruiting and retention. They have a tight team, and people love serving in this unit, myself included. Many of their airmen today are following in the footsteps of family members. I care deeply for this unit and relish my time commanding from 2016 to 2017.

When the Air Force decided to convert the unit from a C-130 flying unit to becoming the first cyberspace wing, I sensed the need to address the wing in person. I knew this would be emotional for the unit and the community and wanted to show my support. Over one thousand airmen and their families were impacted by a decision they couldn't control. Even though rumors preceded the official announcement, the pain of hearing the message would be too difficult to accept.

When I walked into the crowded "standing room only" auditorium, everyone knew the purpose of my visit. Many would be forced to retire, relocate, resign, or go through the strenuous process of retraining. Either way, this devoted group of professionals, who had committed most of their career to the C-130 mission, were now facing an uncertain future.

Before starting the meeting, I concentrated on the perfect scenario for Ohio and the Air Force. I wanted everyone's agreement to stay in uniform and trust the process of converting to a new mission. The problems standing in the way of this were too numerous to count. The new mission wasn't clearly defined due to the level of secrecy. This base would become the first of its kind, and the timeline for the conversion was still a moving target. To make matters worse, the Department of Defense's budget to pay for the conversion was still in question.

These people had little to count on. I did not have the answers to their difficult questions like, "What's going to happen to me?" "Will I be able to convert to the new mission?" "Will I have to move my family?" "We recently bought a house, and my wife has a job in the community. Should we start looking for jobs in other units, in other states?" "I've trained for the past ten years to become a pilot, and now you're telling me the aircraft are leaving for good. I don't want to become a cyber operator working on a computer. What are you going to do for me?" I walked into a tough crowd, and I wanted everyone to trust me. I wanted them to trust the leaders in the 179th and our staff from headquarters.

I can't forget the faces when I stood in front of the entire team. I remember seeing fear, frustration, anger, and despair. With this much emotion in the room, I didn't expect our people to commit to anything long-term. Instead of pushing for them to stay in the unit, I gave each of them the right to say no. I acknowledged we didn't have enough information. I said I didn't blame them for wanting to leave.

My supporting team from headquarters' human resources, the base leadership team, and other staff members joining me were all in alignment with my plan. We discussed the only way to get past the emotion is to ensure them we would ultimately support their final decision, even if it meant leaving the unit. I worried if too many quit early out of fear, or lacked confidence in our leadership, they might miss out on a great opportunity with the coming mission. Worse, if we lost too many airmen, the Air Force might question our ability to make the transition and close the unit altogether.

Giving those folks the ability to say no brought them closer to making the decision to stay. From the heart I told all of them, "If you decide to leave, I don't blame you. I'll be the first person to write you a letter of recommendation. If you stay with us, however, I promise you the people in this room will be treated fairly. Many of you will be retrained, and I have no doubt you'll look back and be happy you stuck it out. They chose this unit for a reason. You're a resilient team capable of handling change, and the Air Force needs you. This mission will become the tip of the spear for the new combat environment."

This started a yearlong internal negotiation in Ohio. Many who said no in the beginning changed their minds over time.

Only a year later, and after all the aircraft departed for good, the 179th had a ceremony celebrating the start of their new mission. They retired their old unit flag and uniform patches and posted their new colors. What an accomplishment for their leadership team! Far more Airmen than we expected agreed to remain and retrain. Other units in Ohio agreed to absorb those requesting a transfer. Those eligible and asking for early retirement were approved, and a handful took me up on my offer to help them find a position outside of Ohio. Our team took care of everyone.

The senior leadership in the National Guard told us to expect a 25 percent loss in personnel. They predicted this level of attrition based on historical unit conversion data. This combined with extremely low military recruiting numbers in 2022 raised our concerns.[1] We were pleasantly surprised when we only lost 10 percent. In only one year, the unit bounced back and was holding steady at 100 percent manning. I knew letting them initially say no would help them slow down and clearly see their options. Once their emotions were under control, they were able to make better decisions.

Our system is rooted in my father, Jim Camp Sr., believing decisions are 100 percent emotional until a decision is made. In other words, emotions cannot be avoided when you're trying to reach an agreement. When people are negotiating, they tend to fear making a bad decision. Once a decision is made, the transition to logic and intellect begins. Only then can they justify a decision. Jim Sr. used to say the safest decision your opponent can make is to say no. The decision to reject simply maintains the status quo. After years of coaching negotiation, he understood a "no" would lower emotion, and the decider would attempt to validate their decision with intellect. What's brilliant with his insight is how emotions shift back to a more neutral state from the start of the negotiation when the opponent is given the right to veto.[2]

According to Professor Daniel Kahneman, economist, author, and 2002 Nobel Prize winner, once the fear of a potential outcome enters a person's decision-making, their emotions will overcome their ability to think rationally. The more emotional people are, the more difficult it becomes to use logic and intellect.[3]

How do you respond when you're pressured to quickly decide? Have you purchased something out of excitement then quickly regretted it? Applying pressure in hopes of "closing" the deal is a common negotiation practice today, especially in sales. Unfortunately, from our experience in coaching, this tactic increases emotions and delays decisions. Pushing too hard will only raise objections. How many times have you been pressured and said, "Give me time. I need to think."

REASONS PEOPLE SAY NO

In our system of negotiation, no closing pressure is required. We see this pressure frequently in the world of procurement. Usually on behalf of the CEO, procurement professionals are constantly trying to reduce costs in the supply chain. While we understand this is their primary purpose, applying pressure by threatening to switch suppliers is a widely used tactic. The clients we coach often hear statements like, "You better sharpen your pencil on this deal." Many of our clients have admitted before starting to work with Camp Negotiations, out of habit, they would respond to this pressure by offering price concessions.

Unfortunately, if you start caving in, the situation will only get worse. Compromise is a slippery slope, and once you start giving things up in a deal, the other side will keep coming back for more. When our clients hold firm on price and give the procurement teams the right to say no, they find themselves in a great position to uncover what's behind their decision. Ironically, price is rarely the biggest issue.

After over twenty years of negotiation coaching, my brother, Todd Camp, has identified four main reasons why people say no. Here's Todd's perspective:

> As our clients begin to prosecute the list of four reasons, they discover what's truly preventing an agreement. Although pricing is important, there is always more to the deal than price. The first and most common reason people say no is because they lack the emotional vision of the benefit of saying yes. In other words, they may not see what you're offering as a solution to their problems. What it is about our product or service that separates them from their competition?
>
> The second reason they might say no is that they lack the data necessary to support their decision. Perhaps they haven't seen the data, or we haven't provided the right information to support what we're asking them to agree to.
>
> The third, especially when dealing with a procurement professional, is that they lack the

authority to say yes. They can demand a lower price, but ultimately, we may not be working with the entire decision-making team.

The final reason people say no is my favorite: They're bluffing or using "no" as a tactic. They want to see how we react.

Sometimes a "no" can be one or even a combination of all these reasons. Breaking down our opponents' decisions using this list is a great way to keep our emotions under control. We simply keep working on the deal until we reach the real problem. Decisions are made to solve problems, and a "no" is nothing to be afraid of; it's an opportunity.

Whether you're leading a negotiation team working with procurement or delivering bad news to your organization, be aware of the emotions surrounding decisions on both sides of the table. When you see someone getting emotional, try to remain calm and respectful. Don't take it personally. When you have an opportunity, try giving a person the right to say no. You'll quickly see a change in their posture.

The same is true when working internally with your team. The most effective leaders I've seen encourage feedback from their team, even if the feedback is negative. Understand how your teams' emotions can disrupt logical decisions. I'm not suggesting a leader tolerate disrespectful behavior. When you're willing to listen, and not be upset by what you're hearing, you're building trust.

Reflecting on my leadership experiences, you must keep your emotions under control and be willing to hear the word "no." Helping your opponent or teammates reach a decision is predicated on the clarity of vision you create. In our system, vision drives decisions. The stronger the emotions, the more challenging it becomes for anyone to maintain focus and employ rational thought. Emotions cloud vision. Simply pushing a mandate to your team, making perfect sense to you, might not be effective. Ideally, you want your team to see what you see. This is possible if you can manage the emotions in the room.

Remember, in any negotiation, your opponent's vision, not yours, is the key to their decision making. During the negotiation process itself, internal or external, the name of the game is to understand what your opponent sees. What decisions will they have to make, and what emotions are a part of their decision? Taking this posture and focusing on their vision helps them realize what they're sharing with you is important. They'll see you're really listening. This alone will lower their emotions and give you a better chance of reaching an agreement. Don't assume what the real issues are. Ask questions and listen.

CHAPTER 4

CONNECTION IS THE FIRST NEGOTIATION

Organizations evolving at a fast pace are more likely to seek leadership talent with broad experiences. Although tenure and stability are important, a fresh perspective might be necessary to lead others through the process of change.

Leading up to my change of command ceremony in June of 2016, I had numerous opportunities with many leaders to discuss the challenges I would face taking command of the 179th airlift wing in Mansfield, Ohio. First, I replaced a well-liked and charismatic wing commander, Colonel Gary McCue. Gary guided his team for over six years. He grew up in the unit, and with a thirty-plus-year career, he managed to command at each level. He'd also amassed thousands of flying hours, many of those on combat deployments. Gary led from the front and would be missed by his team. I'm not surprised he's still serving and was recently promoted to major general.

Outside of a few group commanders and the vice wing commander all sharing my rank of colonel, nobody knew me. My previous twenty-six years were spent serving elsewhere. I walked in as a complete outsider, which is unusual in the Air National Guard. Normally commanders were home grown and promoted from within. My selection meant I stepped into the top position over others already in line for the job. This created immediate friction. I knew this would be difficult from day one. Speaking of my first day on the job... Gary made sure to hide the keys to my office before he headed off to serve at the National Guard Bureau in Washington, DC. In addition to offering me great advice and support during my transition, he also had a great sense of humor.

My boss at the time, (retired) Major General Mark Bartman, the adjutant general for Ohio, provided clear expectations for my command. He stressed his number one concern was getting the unit through their upcoming inspection. On a five-year schedule, the Air Force would send a team of over fifty personnel to perform a comprehensive unit inspection. In addition to compliance with policy and regulations, they examined culture, managing resources, and the overall effectiveness of the leadership team. We had exactly one year to prepare.

What I didn't know before stepping into my new role was we were on a course to fail the inspection. The unit had gone through the process of changing aircraft from C-130s to C-27s, and then back to C-130s again. We were also identified for base closure. When a unit's going through this kind of turmoil, the last thing on their minds is an inspection. Their focus was keeping the doors open. We had a lot of work to do in a short period. In addition to personally qualifying in the C-130 aircraft, half of the wing had recently deployed to the Middle East.

How do I connect with my new team while also putting together a strategic plan? This plan needed to demonstrate our ability to do the mission, establish a good culture, professionally develop our airmen, and ensure compliance with Air Force regulations. How do you build a strategy, or in our system of negotiation, develop a mission and purpose (M&P) for your team, when you can't find your office key on the first day?

Quickly realizing daily life included leadership negotiation, I reverted to my habit of preparation. Either in my head or on a white board in my office, I couldn't help but develop a negotiation "checklist and log" before and after meetings. Exactly like we coach our clients at Camp Negotiations, the first step on our checklist is developing a mission and purpose. Before attempting this, I realized discovering my new environment would help. During my first week on the job, we had numerous meetings orienting me to all aspects of the mission. Additionally, I attended staff meetings across the base, introducing me to key personnel.

The Friday afternoon at the end of my first week, I requested a private meeting with my new executive officer. When I asked for her perspective on my first week, she hesitated to give me a candid answer. I put her at ease and assured her I really wanted her honest opinion. She relaxed and told me the unit is probably not telling me everything I needed to hear. My team didn't know me, and this would be my first challenge. Instead of continuing with large meetings, which is the standard for incoming leaders, together we decided to take a different approach.

With hundreds of personnel on base in a full-time capacity, we filled up my daily calendar with one-on-one meetings. The best way to explore a new culture is to get to know the people. For the next thirty days, I met privately with everyone regardless of their rank or job. After brief introductions, I asked for their agreement to share: "I need your help today. Tell me what I need to know. What's your impression of this unit?" I also took time to discuss their families, career backgrounds, and future aspirations. They talked, and I listened.

When you don't know the environment, you have a great advantage. Instead of making assumptions, you have the chance to hear it straight from your team. They told me everything I wanted to hear. During our time together, I also had the chance to set an agenda by discussing my leadership priorities. In return for sharing their vision, I made sure to share everything they wanted to know about me. I encouraged them to identify problems, and I took notes when they spoke. They quickly figured out I worked for them, not the opposite. I made sure they knew firsthand my willingness to hear honest feedback. Asking for true opinions helped them realize their importance to the future of our unit. After our one-on-one meetings, things I shared privately permeated the rest of the base. Trust can be established through short internal negotiations. I got to know the people and culture, and they discovered I truly cared.

Passing our inspection relied on the team's ability to align and agree on a shared strategy. Reaching this understanding necessitated many difficult conversations. For a small handful of my new teammates, asking them to support our plan didn't work. They were not willing to change and decided to leave the team altogether. We were not willing to compromise on our expectations for individual accountability.

While preparing for the inspection, the most important thing I discovered is I didn't have all the answers. Although I understood what the inspection team would look for, I didn't have the expertise in all the functions supporting the flying mission. My small leadership team and I wanted everyone to contribute their ideas without fear. I asked everyone to tell me and our command team no when we were off track. Bad ideas or dumb questions didn't exist. We were all open to suggestions. We've all heard leaders say these things, and our team needed to trust we meant it. Problems were uncovered we didn't know existed, and our approach worked. Addressing and uncovering problems paid off.

GO SLOW TO GO FAST

If you've been secure in your current role for many years, chances are you'll eventually end up walking into a new position or even a new company. New leaders at any level can expect counselling on responsibilities, required tasks, goals and objectives, and overall performance. The measurement of your success is likely based on the results of your new team. Before you attempt to reach agreements with your new group, take the time to research and discover who you're working with. Connect with your team and give them the opportunity to get to know you. Try to get a handle on the culture before implementing your big ideas.

I remember Colonel Gary McCue giving me the same advice when I took command of his unit. After serving together at headquarters for five years, we'd become good friends. He had this to say regarding the importance of connecting quickly with your team:

> Connection with members is *the* most important aspect of leadership. Creating a bond is necessary for trust. Trust is necessary for success. If folks do not have trust (or lose trust), the organization will not be successful, period. As an example, when our unit was faced with closure—twice—this trust was the bedrock for weathering the uncertainty. Standing in front of a wing of 1,100 folks and asking for their trust during the crisis would have been folly. We needed trust long before the anxiety of change hit us. Credibility is the trait needed for such situations, and connecting with folks is what secures it.

Conventional wisdom may tell you to "hit the ground running." Take pause before you move out on your well-articulated thirty-, sixty-, or ninety-day plan you might have outlined during your interview. Regardless of why you were selected and your incoming strategy for change, new leaders can be derailed quickly by the existing culture.[1]

Be careful of making a big splash. One of my instructors in Air Force Personnel Officer school used this analogy, and it stuck with me:

> When you're a new leader, imagine you're a new fixture submersing into a fish tank. If you jump hard and fast, the fish will stop swimming in their normal patterns. When you hit the bottom, you'll stir up all the sediment and cloud the water. If you go in slowly and gently, you'll be unnoticed. The fish will keep up their normal patterns, and you can observe more easily. When a new fish swims by, take the opportunity to engage with them and understand their environment. Try to discover the world they live in. Keep in mind they may not be happy you're there in the first place.

The first agreement you should make is you want their help. Let them know their perspectives are extremely valuable. This will build immediate trust.

The majority of your new teammates have been there long before your arrival. You have a unique opportunity to build trust. By asking your new coworkers to help you understand this new environment, you can begin to uncover who they are and what problems or challenges they see. If you're their new boss, they'll most likely expect you to share your vision and expectations.

When you're tempted to do this, slow down and get connected first.

The connection is a two-way street. Let your guard down a little and give them the chance to understand who you are and what's important to you. Walk in slowly and carve out time to get to know the people next to you, especially your subordinates. Your one-on-one leadership negotiations with each member will lead to collective results.

A new leader building their own team from scratch is rare. Time permitting, the same caution applies. During a recent talk with my son-in-law, Sixto, he said he's being asked to build and lead a national business development team. He's been selling high-end electronic components for the manufacturing industry for the past few years. In addition to being accountable for his own performance, he'll be responsible for the success of his team. Moving from an autonomous role in sales to leadership is exciting, and his concerns of managing others is natural.

I shared with him the importance of choosing his players. While credentials and experience of his candidates should be considered, his ability to connect with them is more important. I suggested letting these folks get to know him and help them see how he'll support them. In taking this approach, a door will open. I also emphasized for Sixto to take his time and find the perfect fit. Find those willing to help you build the culture you're trying to create. The decision to hire someone is important, and putting more effort into this first negotiation will pay off long term. At the end of our conversation, he realized this would be more difficult than he expected. He also shared this would probably be easier than taking over an existing team.

When companies hire our coaches at Camp Negotiations, we're often brought into deals mid-stream. In fact, most of our clients seek advice when negotiations are in trouble. Imagine you're on a company video call preparing for a big negotiation, and unfamiliar faces appear. Who are these coaches, and why are they involved? If we haven't had the chance to meet the teams we're coaching in person, a period of awkwardness is normal. After brief introductions, we make a point to take a position of observation. Before we can offer guidance and lead their team in critical negotiations, we take our time getting to know our clients. This can be a big challenge. Although their company leadership decided to bring us in, the team's willingness to share their challenges is not a given.

Over the past year, I've had the opportunity to work side-by-side with our partner and coach, Dave DeSantis. Dave has an extensive business background serving many companies in C-level positions. Dave recently shared his thoughts on the challenges of coaching a new team:

> While as coaches we know the "what" that needs to be accomplished, which is helping them negotiate more successful outcomes, we must give our clients the chance to walk their own decision path and not tell them what

to do. Some require more time than others deciding to let us help. Hopefully, we have the time to connect to a few individuals before addressing their entire group. Those one-on-one connections where we can begin to understand their environment gives a coach the ability to determine *when* it's best to start coaching and *how* we can best structure our support to most effectively meet their needs.

From a position of humility, it's important to understand their personal negotiation experiences. Before you make the ultimate ask to offer your coaching help, you must build trust and demonstrate you're cut from a similar cloth. If you can connect with one or two people in the room, you'll see others begin to engage. A couple of wins creates the social proof our coaching can help. Taking the time to start slowly with the personal connections helps the rest of the team go faster.

When you're a newly anointed leader, whether you've been brought in from the outside, promoted internally, or building an entirely new team, take the time to research and get to the people and culture. Prevent assumptions from interfering with your decision making by approaching with a blank slate. Before trying to negotiate big changes internally, connect and build trust. If you want people to tell you the truth, show them you're willing to listen before pushing too hard with your new ideas. Before you try presenting a solution to a big problem, remember three things:

- Ask yourself, "What do I want my team to see and discover?"
- Focus on how they'll benefit from solutions you want to deliver to the team.
- Seek to understand their world, and really listen to what people are telling you.

Moving into the structure of our negotiation system, you'll find the above list builds a foundation for developing your mission and purpose for negotiation.

CHECKLIST STEP 1: MISSION AND PURPOSE— THE FOUNDATION FOR NEGOTIATION

In the world of negotiation, your perceived "need" to reach an agreement is relative to the importance of the end results. The higher the stakes, the more you're willing to commit. When the scope and importance of a deal increases, the big question becomes how and where to devote your energy. Although establishing team alignment on the desired outcome is important, keep in mind you can't control the decisions of others. If you're not careful, emotions will take over and inhibit your ability to find out what's important for the other side. Pushing too hard for a mutually beneficial win-win solution, or trying to use leverage forcing an agreement, can backfire. Your "need" will be seen by your opposition. Need is a vulnerability and will delay or completely blow your agreement.

If the negotiation you're working on is critical, preparing a checklist starting with your overall mission and purpose will help you shift focus away from results. This will improve your chance of success. Don't waste your energy and emotions agonizing over results.

My father was correct when he said, "You cannot control results in any negotiation. You cannot manage your wins and losses. The only thing you can control is your activity and your behavior."[1]

Taking the time to develop a M&P is a worthwhile activity. Simply ask yourself: What do I want my employee or potential client to discover? How will they benefit from what I'm asking them to agree to? Recalling our definition of negotiation, the real effort to reach agreement is preparation and how you behave during the negotiation. Seeking to understand your opponent's vision and decision-making before you start presenting solutions is not easy. Mission and purpose will keep you grounded in their world. Agreements are routed in your ability to help them see and discover what you want to provide, how you want to deliver it, and how they'll benefit.

In the previous chapter, I mentioned the big Air Force inspection and how critical the results would be to the future of our base in Mansfield, Ohio. With a mostly new command team, we had little time to prepare. Failing the inspection became too difficult to discuss. The commanders and supervisors across the base knew our jobs were on the line. Instead of fixating on the "need" for results, we took a different approach. We wanted the entire base to "see and discover" what it would take to put forth our best effort. Our virtual inspection leading up to the main event occurred one year before my arrival, and the feedback concerned all of us. With too many challenges to address, I'll admit the pressure overwhelmed me. My main challenge, aside from mentally keeping it together, was getting everyone aligned on how we would prepare. This would require tight agreement across the base. Without it, we had no chance.

Me giving orders would not make us successful. I couldn't force people to follow me. During our first town-hall meeting, I made sure everyone knew the end results were my responsibility. I would protect everyone and take the hit if we didn't pass. Remember, you can't force a team to buy-in to your vision. You cannot control the decision making of others. You can't give direct orders too often and expect to maintain trust and cohesion.

I not only wanted these folks to stay with us, I also wanted our airmen to improve their respective squadrons for the future. The federal funding and the Air Force's overall confidence in the unit was at stake. My mission and purpose intended to help the entire base discover the importance of personal accountability. By allowing our practice inspection teams from other units to identify where we were falling short of the Air Force standards, we could remedy lasting solutions. Those newly implemented procedures and programs would hold everyone accountable regardless of rank or position. Everyone needed to accept responsibility and openly admit where we were broken.

The common tendency for any team is to quantify what they do well. Most leaders want to laud their team's accomplishments versus admitting where they need to improve. The key to passing this inspection meant everyone needed to risk their own reputation. Our leaders had to embrace the red and come clean. They needed to get comfortable disagreeing with each other. The leadership in each section of the base knew their team. They also knew what needed fixed. Our agenda had to encourage and reward their willingness to expose their weaknesses. This meant trusting their leadership wouldn't penalize them for admitting where they needed help. At first, we witnessed tremendous pushback. Conversations and decisions were difficult. Teams having the courage to look at each other and admit, "No, we are not where we should be," isn't easy.

After months of preparation, and in line with our M&P, we all agreed to conduct our own self-inspection before the real thing. We knew exactly where the inspection team would be looking and what they'd be looking for. We decided to hold ourselves accountable and send our results to their leader two weeks in advance of the inspection team. This practice is not standard, and it surprised the inspection team. Our M&P guided our decisions and actions leading up to the inspection. More importantly, it brought the whole team together.

Unfortunately, one of our squadron commanders rejected our M&P, and we replaced him one week before the event.

When the general and his team arrived, he said we were the first base to take this approach. No other unit delivered such a thorough report self-identifying areas of weakness. He appreciated our candor. In my eight-hour interview with the team chief, he informed me they were initially expecting the 179th Airlift Wing to fail the inspection. The opposite happened during their visit. Because we clearly identified our own deficiencies in each section of our base and demonstrated a clear plan for remediation, we passed the inspection.

This was a huge win for the entire team. The general in charge of the inspection team sent a note to the entire Air Force proclaiming our culture of accountability. We were ready for combat, and we had a solid leadership team shaping the future of the unit.

Looking back on the months of preparation, we focused on what we could control—ourselves. Of course, the desired results were always in the back of our minds. But we didn't become consumed by our need to succeed. Although this may seem like a high-pressure leadership negotiation, it probably fails in comparison to what many business leaders experience.

The strategy within a venture-backed start-up is always focused on innovation and growth. The result of a successful strategy can lead to acquisition, which is usually the ultimate win for these companies. Can you imagine the CEO's pressure to produce results?

My brother, Todd Camp, who I previously mentioned, has coached negotiation in the mergers and acquisitions arena for years. He had this to say when we discussed mission and purpose:

> You know, the most important negotiations happen internally with start-ups. Using our system and focusing on mission and purpose has always been our coaching focus. We concentrate on what it is we're trying to provide and how we provide it to the benefit of our opponent. Everything's founded on mission and purpose, so even when the start-up team is talking about negotiating with their board, or even their investors, they're thinking about what they provide that's absolutely in their opponent's world and how the opponent benefits. We can't afford to worry about how we would benefit from any deal. Worrying about the results is like pouring gasoline on an emotional fire that's already almost out of control.
>
> When they're preparing for a big negotiation, you can see relationships internally get stronger, not weaker. Even if it's a tough conversation, whether the team agrees or disagrees, you see the respect the team has for the leader go up

dramatically. The tension in those teams is a positive thing. Everyone becomes laser focused on the mission and purpose.

We have seen a lot of times where the CEO's team members have a better idea, or a better plan, or a better strategy. The CEOs are so dug into the potential results, and they're under so much pressure, that they can't take the time to think outside the box. They can't think beyond their current position and stake in the company. I think our system's also a good way to build younger leaders. They learn how to focus and prepare with a system. This keeps the team on an even keel, and the focus shifts from money to preparation and their mission and purpose.

MISSION AND PURPOSE HELPS MANAGE THE "NEED" FOR RESULTS

In addition to our son James, my wife Cynthia and I have three daughters, Jordan, Brittany, and Remy. Jordan and Remy are both college softball players and examples of managing the need for results. Imagine what goes through their minds when they walk up to the plate. Both will tell you from experience a secure spot in the lineup doesn't exist. If you don't produce in the batter's box, you'll ride the bench.

My oldest, Jordan, before walking up to the plate, reads a saying on a note card or sings a song in her head to distract her from the pressures of getting on base. My youngest daughter, Remy, who's currently a junior at Warner University in Florida, smiles and reminds herself of a funny softball memory from years ago. Depending on the game situation, controlling the self-induced pressure to get a hit is a big challenge for any batter. Nobody wants to let their team down. Imagine if everyone in the dugout, especially their coaches, demanded a hit. Does this help them focus on swinging at a good pitch? If negotiation, like softball, is a human performance event, controlling the need for results is a must.

If you're in a position of leadership, chances are you won't be there for too long if you don't produce results. The inherent leadership pressure tied to performance is always there. Let's look at the sales world. Sales negotiations can take months to put together with hundreds of decisions along the way. For those of you with experience selling a product or service, you know the ups, downs, and uncertainties can take their toll on your emotions. From my experience coaching in sales negotiations, the fear of rejection, or the fear of hearing the word "no," or "striking out," is the biggest reason people leave a sales job. If a salesperson attaches their own self-image with their lack of results, the chances of them surviving in sales are slim. On the other hand, when someone honestly believes in their product or service, they might stick it out and succeed.

When you can let go of results and understand you can't control the decisions of others, you won't be impacted personally when you hear no. Sadly, I've encountered numerous sales managers who do a poor job of coaching their people. They manage their teams and push for results by using intimidation and fear. One would hope a sales leader would act more like a coach in athletics. Practice with your team, teach them fundamentals, give them a game plan for success, motivate the team when times are difficult... You get my point. The truth is this: A coaching approach to leading a sales team doesn't happen often enough. Too much focus rests on results, getting the win, and closing the deal and not enough on helping their sales team develop a mission and purpose.

One of our top negotiation coaches, Mark Glenewinkel, uses this example to help sales professionals conceptualize M&P:

> Picture a doctor's office with a room full of patients. When the doctor meets with each patient, he or she begins a process of discovery. The ultimate "result" the doctor is trying to achieve is helping each patient to improve their health. The doctor is not trying to "sell" the patient an expensive medical procedure. That would be morally and ethically inappropriate until the doctor has a complete picture of the patient's medical history, blood work, lifestyle, and tests. More importantly, the patient and doctor must reach an agreement on the proper diagnosis and treatment options before any decisions are made.

The doctor is completely focused on delivering the proper advice and treatment options that are 100 percent to the benefit of the patients. I can't think of a more profound example of a good mission and purpose. The doctor *wants* the patient to be healthy and is willing to deliver what's required. Unfortunately, not all patients will reach an agreement to follow the doctor's advice. The patient may say no to a host of suggestions, but the doctor still has a room full of patients he's trying to help. Sales become easier when you visualize your potential clients as a room full of patients.

Creating a mission and purpose is the foundation of our negotiation system. We coach our clients to develop an overall M&P for each negotiation. Since negotiations may require multiple engagements with their opponent, the mission and purpose may change for each interaction. This is the most important aspect in preparing for any negotiation, internal or external.

What I discovered leading people is how well the concept of M&P supports reaching an agreement within your team. When you focus on the success of your team and sincerely seek to understand their world, they'll trust you and let you in. If you're uncovering how they see challenging situations, you can identify where to devote your effort. In a leadership negotiation, you'll know you're on a good track when problems start surfacing. When this happens, you may be tempted to avoid problems and reach for the result. Dealing with problems up front in any deal may seem counterintuitive. The reality is problems don't simply vanish. Ignoring problems is another way of giving in to your need for results. This is why identifying problems is the next step in our system of negotiation.

CHAPTER 6

CHECKLIST STEP 2: PROBLEMS AND BAGGAGE

Reflect for a moment on your decision to join your current company or organization. When you interviewed for this position, were you negotiating? Why did you take the job? Why did they hire you?

Job candidates and employers are always searching for the perfect fit. Each does their best to look like an attractive option. The company's job announcement typically includes a salary range, benefits package, and overall summary of the position. Candidates polish up their résumés and line up references. Both are conducting research and may turn to recruiting services to help narrow their search. Leading up to the interview, the process is open and transparent. Matching a person to the perfect job may seem easy to someone who hasn't experienced the frustration of the game. For those of us who have participated, we know how hard this can be.

Both you and your employer must have seen a mutual opportunity if you decided to interview. During the interview, were they simply validating everything on your résumé, or were they trying to dig deeper to find issues they couldn't see on the surface? Considering your future employer, what questions did you have? After the interview, you could have walked away from their offer, and your employer could have selected another person. Before you took their offer, how many challenges needed solving?

Perhaps you had to relocate your family or wanted to negotiate a higher salary. When you and your employer finally shook hands and agreed, what made the difference? Maybe you both seized the chance to solve a big underlying problem. They needed someone like you on their team, and you were looking for a good team to join. In the entire hiring process, how many issues did both sides address? Using this example, I would argue most complex agreements are a collection of decisions to solve problems.

DEAL WITH PROBLEMS EARLY

The strongest agreements occur when problems are dealt with early in the deal. In our system of negotiation, we embrace the biggest problems from the start. This is why the second step in our negotiation checklist, after mission and purpose, is uncovering and addressing problems. We prepare for the negotiation by rank ordering any problems we're aware of. Starting with the most significant, we make internal decisions and seek them from those we're negotiating with. This is required to keep the deal moving. Like an employer looking for employees with the required level of education and experience, if we can't get past a major problem, the agreement will not happen.

I realize using the word "problem" may imply a negative connotation. This is not my intent. A problem is simply a challenge or issue interfering with decision-making. Solving problems is an opportunity to strengthen a deal. Although ignoring issues won't necessarily kill a deal in the beginning, you might get lucky. What if they surface later? Avoiding issues up front can jeopardize your deal in the long run.

We see this frequently while coaching business negotiations. Clients get excited picturing an early win only to watch it fall apart when they try to finalize terms and conditions. Problems rarely go away on their own. Neglected issues can resurface. Especially with people, they'll fester and force decisions which cannot be reversed. We've all seen this in the workplace. A leader not aware of or unwilling to tackle problems when they appear will face an even bigger challenge when their team starts to vote with their feet. The moment you or your coworkers start looking for another company, it might be too late for anyone to talk you into staying.

Avoiding or failing to address issues in external negotiations is also a terrible mistake. This can result in dissolved contracts, failed relationships, and litigation. Looking at the stressors on the economy from 2020 to 2023, to say new challenges have emerged negatively impacting business agreements is an understatement. The combination of a global pandemic and overall inflation has not only stressed the average consumer, the B2B world has also encountered countless problems. Managing their workforce, maintaining cashflow, protecting margins, and maintaining healthy business relationships have necessitated more flexibility than usual. Negotiated agreements once taken for granted became suspect. Stable issues before COVID-19, like fulfillment, terms and conditions, and pricing, became joepardized.[1]

While working with a recent client, the CEO we supported shared his frustration with one of his major customers. They were locked into a five-year contract where the terms and conditions of the agreement had no provisions for increased costs due to issues like the pandemic or inflation. While the CEO didn't engage in the negotiation himself, he knew his team managing the deal were frustrated. Instead of their customer's willingness to address our client's increasing costs to produce and deliver the product, which they needed desperately, the customer refused to negotiate. They stated, "Your rising costs are not our problem." The customer also routinely bullied our client's account managers over frivolous delivery issues. They probably perceived having "leverage" over our client and the upper hand in the existing contract.

With the existing contract expiring soon, our client received a proposal seeking a new deal for the production and delivery of another key product. The opposition's procurement team, previously refusing to work with our clients, were suddenly ready to negotiate. With a year remaining in their current contract, our CEO decided to reject their offer altogether. Based on the feedback from his team, and the customers' unwillingness to renegotiate during unprecedented times in the economy, the customers found themselves without a supplier. In a plea of desperation after our client told them no to a future deal of any kind, they were now willing to provide reparations on the previous deal. Backed into a corner, they were willing to address the "problems" of the previous contract. I wonder who will have the advantage if the CEO decides to counter their new proposal?

The problems you dismiss can also damage business relationships. If the aforementioned business deal does continue, our coaching clients may have to cope with the "emotional baggage" they carry. Their frustrations in dealing with a difficult customer may be too much to forgive. The problems ignored, regardless for who's responsible, can lead to bigger issues negotiating future deals.

EMOTIONAL BAGGAGE CAN BECOME A PROBLEM

When you're preparing for negotiation, you must consider the potential for emotional baggage. For example, let's suppose you're the hiring official bringing on a new employee or promoting someone from within the organization. What's your firsthand knowledge or perception of the candidate? Maybe you've heard rumors, or you've had a bad experience working with this person in the past. How could this interfere with your decision? Conversely, how does the candidate view your company? Perhaps you've turned them down in previous interviews, or they've read bad press in the media implicating your company. Emotional baggage is a potential problem you should be aware of.

Growing up in a flying squadron surrounded by strong personalities, I've seen plenty of heated disagreements during a flight debriefing. I'm not going to lie; I can remember those confrontations like they were yesterday. Our squadron had an understanding: What's said in the debrief stays in the debrief. I've gone toe-to-toe with some of my closest military teammates in the past, and we don't let those arguments interfere with our jobs or friendship.

Baggage becomes a problem when we can't "put it down" by getting over history or perceptions. If you build a negotiation checklist, baggage is something you should look at closely. This way, you're not caught off guard if it becomes an issue.

After serving in the military for a long time, I've developed my own personal baggage when it comes to swearing in new recruits. Don't get me wrong, I've had no better honor than to see a young person willing to take the oath of enlistment. This is the first and most important agreement a new teammate makes. Saying those words, "To support and defend the constitution," is a big deal.

I've seen too many military careers end early due to bad decision-making and uninformed expectations. Because of this, I make the effort to meet with the recruit and their family before the official enlistment. The recruiters in Ohio are used to this, because they know I'm going to emphasize the expectations and the potential problems that could interfere with honorable service. On occasion, I've had family members, and even the recruits themselves, back out of joining at the last minute. We only want people to join who are fully aware of the terms and their enlistment agreement. Having them change their minds after they've reported to basic training is not in line with the mission and purpose I have for a recruit.

When I ask them, "What makes you want to join the military?" I've heard a variety of answers. I had a mother speak up one day and say, "This is the only way we can pay for our daughter's college." I acknowledged what a great benefit this was for their family and then asked the most important question for any parent: "Do you understand regardless of their military specialty, your son or daughter will most likely deploy during their term of service?" If this certainty is not put on the table up front, then *I* blew it when they don't show up for deployment.

One of the most difficult commander duties is signing a discharge package, thereby kicking someone out of the military. They'll have a mark on their permanent record and may even have to pay back tens of thousands of dollars in college aid for not fulfilling their service agreement. I always say before they take the oath, "If you're going to break this agreement in the future, you're better off to leave now." I know this sounds harsh. I want them to understand reality. Leaving the military with a less than honorable discharge is hard to overcome.

My hands are tied most of the time, and I have no option other than kicking them out. A bad decision leads to punishment. If the airman's worthy of a second chance, and the regulations permit, I use progressive discipline and offer the airman a second chance. I've always been inclined to handle personnel issues with optimism. I truly want all airmen to reach their full potential. Sadly, I've had to remove many from our ranks. When this happens, my team and I look internally to make sure we didn't ignore problems we could have avoided. I ask myself, "Did we know the airman well enough to know when he or she started having issues?" I believe if you don't know what a good day looks like, how can you recognize when your teammates are having a bad day?

GOOD LEADERS WELCOME PROBLEMS

Brigadier General Kenny Maynus, a good friend and military colleague, recently discussed the challenges of leadership. When comparing leadership problems we've both dealt with, he said: "Leadership and taking care of your people is like swimming upstream. The moment you find yourself coasting along and drifting with the current, it's probably time to get out of the river."

I agree with his assessment. While talking with fellow leaders and those I've mentored, all admit the steady flow of problems are endless. Especially when it comes to managing people, dealing with difficult issues is the norm. I've always encouraged an open door policy. This means I'm always willing to assist, even when the solution creates tension or conflict. From my experience observing other leaders, when your teammates stop bringing you their problems, you may have an even bigger issue. If your team senses you don't have the energy or are not approachable, you're on the verge of losing their loyalty and trust. If you're not completely devoted to seeking resolutions for your team, you may need to consider stepping down. Problems consume most of a leader's energy.

The success of your organization is highly dependent on the success of each member of your team. Success with employees relies on employee engagement and the level of care you show to your teammates. Unfortunately, in today's environment, having people dedicated to the mission of an organization is not enough. Without loyalty between the leaders and teammates, performance will break down when the going gets tough.[2] If you lead people, problems can and will surface, jeopardizing the effectiveness of your organization. When it comes to your people, the way you address hard situations can strengthen agreements, build trust, and reveal opportunities to improve the culture.

Undoubtedly, challenges will arise demanding your immediate attention and decisive action. When you suspect an issue, or catch wind of one developing, take a pause if time permits. Especially if you're a young leader, be careful of jumping the gun and making assumptions. Slow down and shift into a mode of discovery. Be sure to ask questions and conduct your research before deciding how to act. The same applies during a negotiation. When you discover an issue exists, ask open-ended questions, or "interrogative-led" questions, to uncover the validity of your concerns.

DELEGATE PROBLEMS AND
TRUST YOUR TEAMMATES

In 2017, during a diplomatic visit to Belgrade, Serbia, our leadership team from Ohio had dinner with Serbia's top military officers. The Ohio National Guard and Serbia are military partners. Having frequent engagements each year is an important part of preserving our relationship. Before this trip, I recently took command of the Ohio Air National Guard. This was my first chance to meet our partners in my new role.

After meeting their commanding general and chief of defense, he asked me a question in front of the whole delegation: "You're a new commander. You have more responsibility. What have you learned in your new position?" The table got quiet, and my team from Ohio all smiled. I guess they expected him to put me on the spot. I responded with an unscripted and genuine answer: "The more leadership responsibility you have, the more you need to trust and empower your team. You must delegate problems to people you work with and trust."

Leaders cannot be in all places. If an organization has many levels of leadership and supervision, the C-level executives need more than reports and metrics. The first-line employees must be able to push problems up the chain and know they'll be handled. Although many things should be handled at the lowest level possible, when you're in doubt, you need to have confidence to elevate the issue to a higher level. If you're the boss, this is probably the most fundamental agreement you need to establish. Problems allowed to fester will only grow and damage your team. I've often said to my commanders across the state, "Leadership is a team sport. If you have a challenge or encounter a problem you're struggling with, please reach out to your fellow commanders or myself. Don't make hard decisions alone. Spread the decision and get help."

We can also create problems ourselves. If you're leading an internal negotiation with your team, or you make a mistake while trying to land a big business deal, own it. Effective negotiators find a respectful way to tell the truth and take responsibility when they drop the ball. I've rarely been involved in a leadership negotiation or coached in a negotiation where everything follows our plan.

Indecision on either side doesn't advance your agreement. Make your decisions and seek the decisions of others to solve challenges. Don't be afraid of saying or hearing the word "no." A "no" is simply a decision that can change. I know you want results. Forget the results and focus on the decisions you want along the way. This will keep you on track to get what you want. You should identify the decisions you want before each negotiation event. This is the next step in our preparation checklist.

CHAPTER 7

CHECKLIST STEP 3: DECISIONS YOU WANT

The third step on our checklist is where you identify the decisions you want your opponent to make and communicate the decisions you've reached.

The longer you work in a leadership role, the less surprised you'll be when someone on your team makes a decision you didn't expect. People change their minds all the time. The same is true when it comes to negotiation. If you do either long enough, you'll begin to protect yourself emotionally by managing expectations. A quick or easy "yes" is nothing to get excited over, the word "maybe" doesn't bring you closer to an agreement, and you don't get discouraged when you hear no. I've rarely coached or participated in a negotiation where a final or lasting decision comes easy.

Rather than seeking the decisions they want from their team, leaders can be tempted to make assumptions instead. I made this mistake in 2018. Part of my job commanding the Air National Guard in Ohio was developing leadership talent. To keep track of the command positions across the state, I used a big white board. Like a depth chart used by sports coaches, this created a visual layout of our positions and talent. My small leadership team and I met routinely, speculating the succession planning for known openings. We managed dozens of leadership jobs across ten different locations, and we tried to stay a year ahead of the known transfers and retirements.

During my first few months on the job, I quickly realized what little control we had over our plan. The names earmarked for commander replacements were constantly changing. Despite our best intentions, we were rarely accurate in our predictions. Those we thought would want to move up and promote either had a change of heart or retired. Others we didn't consider as likely candidates surprised us. We couldn't keep up with the unexpected changes because we didn't have insight into our teammate's decisions.

Luckily my team and I figured it out early. Negotiating sooner and more effectively with our folks offered more predictability. Setting an agenda sooner in their careers gave us a better picture of their decision making. Over time this provided more certainty. Sharing decisions became a reciprocal arrangement. We couldn't afford to make empty promises guaranteeing jobs and promotions with our pool of talent; however, we needed to share our vision for their future. Helping people see the options for their career trajectory is important. Unless we negotiated with each person individually, our team would form their own assumptions on where they stood in the organization. By giving our leaders a candid picture of where they stood and future opportunities within the organization, they openly shared their career aspirations.

Strong agreements depend on transparency. The decisions you're after can be unreliable if you can't see the motivation behind them.

WHAT'S DRIVING THE DECISION?

In our system of negotiation, effective decision-making is everything. While decisions from both sides are necessary, the strength of the agreement is more fortified when you understand what's behind those your counterpart is making. In a low-risk setting, the next time someone agrees with you quickly, try saying, "I'm glad you agree with me. What prompted you to say yes?" If they reject what you're suggesting, allow them to say no and follow with a question. "You can certainly tell me no. Help me understand what I'm missing here. For my own benefit, what's the real issue holding you back?" In either case, how they answer gives you valuable insight. Don't be afraid of what you might hear. Embrace it.

When you're preparing this section of your checklist, ask yourself, "What do I want them to reject or accept during this engagement?" Incremental actions are required for negotiations to progress. If they reject or can't decide, you have an opportunity to address a problem. Identify the reasoning for their rejection or indecision. Don't apply pressure, keep their emotions level, and discover why. Ask yourself, "What else can I provide to help with their decision?"

If you hear maybe, be careful. You want an acceptance or rejection in this step, and not "We're getting closer to a decision." Don't allow yourself to fall into the trap of thinking "maybe" is a decision. A "maybe" is not a decision, and you can't afford to think it moves you closer to an agreement. When you hear the word, how do you respond? Do you get excited and think you're closer to a yes, or is it simply a nice way for someone to avoid telling you no? I'm not suggesting you don't give people time to think and process. I'm saying the safest decision you can help someone make, in the moment, is to tell you no. At best, consider a person stuck on a "maybe" is simply saying, "No for the time being."

The next time this happens, try saying, "It seems like you're not ready to make a decision, and you certainly can say, 'No.' What concerns do you have holding you back?" If you continually set an agenda giving the other side the right to veto, you'll be shocked at what you'll discover. Barriers will come down, and they'll share more of what's going on in their mind.

Regardless of what you hear, stay calm and keep your emotions under control. Remain in the other person's world and seek to understand how and why they reached a decision. You can't manage results, and you can't control the decision-making of others. Stay focused on the process uncovering your opponent's vision and not the end game.

Depending on what you find out, this step in our system is also where you communicate your decisions. What you're willing or not willing to do may change if you can learn more from whom you're negotiating with. If you're unsure, slow down and regroup. Your mission and purpose will guide you. If you go too fast, your own decision-making will suffer. If their decision is a deal-breaker for you, how much time, energy, and emotion to you want to waste?

PUSHING TOO HARD FOR A "YES"

From my experience coaching sales negotiations, new clients start out wanting to win and close deals. All they can see is the potential sales commissions. Many assume hearing the word "yes" repeatedly means the deal is getting closer. We help sales professionals discover if they aggressively push for a "yes," they miss out on the opportunity to uncover what's going on with their clients behind the curtain. The problem with moving too quickly and pushing for decisions is they come across needy and lose control of their behaviors and actions.

Reaching an agreement in sales, like other complex negotiations, can require multiple iterations and numerous decisions. One of our coaches, Mark Glenewinkel, reinforced this for me. Mark is an accomplished business executive in the tech industry. Before joining Camp, he led sales teams, became a COO and CFO, and worked in venture capital. When it comes to decisions, he had this to say:

> Like leadership, you want your team or customer to own their decision and execute. No one likes to be told what to do or what to buy. Let me repeat that, *no one* likes to be told what to do. But everyone likes to see, discover, and make their own decisions. Your objective as an effective sales exec or leader is to provide an environment where your customers come to their own conclusions. They

are not doing this because you told or sold them; they are doing it because they own their decision and the outcome. This process drives and builds trust between you, your team, and your customers. You may not close every sales deal, but there is no reason you don't build trust with the people you lead or the customers you serve.

Leading people to reach an agreement is not different from negotiating a sales deal. Controlling the agenda and allowing others to safely make decisions will make you more effective.

SETTING THE AGENDA FOR DECISIONS

In January of 2019, I had the opportunity to participate in a large military exercise in the Pacific. My job was director of Air Mobility Forces advising the four-star general and commander of the Pacific Air Forces. Maneuvering our military assets in the Pacific required an incredible amount of air refueling and airlift missions. Thousands of personnel from all branches in the military participated in this simulated conflict with China. My boss had his hands full with people and assets scattered across the region.

Working with the general during the exercise inspired me. Witnessing his calm demeanor and ability to collaborate with his team is the best leadership I've seen in my military career. He stressed the decisions we made during the exercise provided opportunities to gain experience and improve. He set a clear agenda with the whole team: Regardless of your age, level of experience, or rank, be prepared to share your expertise and contribute. If you were in the back row of the briefing room, or connected to the meeting virtually, be ready to engage in the decision-making process.

From my perspective, the general negotiated with the entire team. Our team's planning and figuring out "what to do" was obviously important in any combat scenario. He also wanted his team to communicate the "how" and the "why." He helped us realize how learning to react to our adversaries' moves would solidify our military's future strategy in the Pacific. He wanted his team to build confidence while making decisions. He also wanted his team to speak up when something didn't look right. The results of his approach made everyone realize their importance in the exercise. They were comfortable providing inputs to solve problems. He challenged the team to contribute without fear. His agenda worked. We ended the training better prepared for the real thing.

A few years later in 2022, the same general visited one of our bases in Ohio. The 179th Airlift Wing in Mansfield was beginning to transition from the C-130 Hercules flying mission to a new cutting-edge mission in cyberspace. His message to the entire Air Force preceded his arrival. Unless we change and adapt quickly to the evolving National Defense Strategy, we will find ourselves at a great disadvantage. The military is shifting from a twenty-year focus on the global war on terror to a global competition with two major countries. This urgent need for change was impacting my former unit in Ohio. I shared his concerns, and I'm grateful he made the trip to see our airmen. The general wanted to communicate with everyone during his visit, expressing how important they were to this new mission. He also set an agenda with the airmen to make decisions.

Before he addressed our team of one thousand, we held a private meeting with state and wing leadership. Our discussion focused on the problems we faced during our mission transition. To meet Air Force timelines, we needed action in the form of decisions. He agreed to support us with stakeholders outside of our reach. He had the horsepower to turn our requests for help into action items at the national level.

When we walked to the hangar for the larger audience, the general took the opportunity to stop and talk with individuals. For many of our airmen, seeing a four-star general in person, let alone shaking his hand while having a short candid discussion, is rare. Everyone appreciated his sincerity during his opening remarks. He needed our help. Observing our folks in the hangar, he formed an instant connection.

He focused on our world and quickly interacted with the audience to understand their challenges. Leading over half a million personnel in active duty, reserves, and the Air National Guard, he negotiated with everyone on base. He and the Air Force headquarters wanted airmen to step up and challenge the typical ways of doing business. If changes would make us more effective in a conflict, he wanted to support those ideas. The decision he wanted was for our team to push new innovative ideas up the chain of command. We all knew he'd have our backs if we decided to follow his lead.

Acknowledging we would face resistance, he encouraged us to not fear the word "no." If someone had a solution to a long-standing problem slowing the process of change, he asked us to not give up elevating a solution. Instead, we were to gather data and respectfully present a course of action making us more agile in combat. If regulations or processes were outdated, he wanted us to speak up. If a process didn't exist, we should develop one.

Challenging the status quo and the bureaucratic decision-making process is the only way to force change. Deciding how to improve and modernize couldn't wait. Paraphrasing his closing remarks, he said, "You'll know when you've succeeded when the first of many 'noes' changes to, 'Why haven't we been doing it this way from the start?'" He not only gave us the ability to say no and challenge the status quo, the general encouraged us not to fear the word.

TEAM ALIGNMENT AND HOLDING FIRM ON YOUR DECISIONS

On a recent coaching call, my brother Todd and I were helping a CEO and his procurement team prepare for a long-term deal with their largest supplier. Our client desperately needed the supplier's materials. Unfortunately, the price for those items increased significantly over time. Our client indicated the relationship between the companies was strong but also had market data suggesting their prices were too high. While helping them build a checklist, we listened to our clients debate over the decisions they wanted from the supplier. The CEO wanted the optimal outcome, which included a full price reduction, while his team suggested they shoot for a partial decrease they could all live with.

The CEO led a collaborative discussion hoping to form alignment. He wanted to stand firm on a full price reduction. Trying not to push too hard on his own views, he asked questions to get the perspectives of the team members working the deal directly. He asked, "What have I missed in the pricing data? How confident are you with the data? Are the numbers accurate? What concerns do you have if we hold firm on price reduction? How comfortable are you with them rejecting our position?" The CEO suggested he'd stay out of the deal until the supplier elevated the decision internally to their senior leadership.

Following our coaching and their CEO's questions, the team reached a consensus. They all wanted the supplier to reject or accept the "optimal" level of cost reduction. The purchasing team responded to their price increases with a respectful no. They simply stated, "We're respectfully rejecting your proposed pricing model." Initially this made our coaching clients uneasy. In the past they would've suggested a lower number to start the process of bargaining. When our team held firm, the supplier rejected the lower pricing for the materials and did exactly what we expected. Despite their initial negative reaction, the supplier quickly compromised and suggested "meeting in the middle." Our team admitted, in the past they would have conceded to the offer for compromise to preserve their long business relationship.

In the next iteration, the CEO and his team held firm again. They thanked the supplier for the offer to reduce prices and again respectfully declined. Our client then suggested an in-person meeting to examine the cost structure of each product while comparing prices to their recent market data. The supplier agreed. In advance of their meeting, they sent a comprehensive price list of the dozens of materials they were trying to sell. Although the previous contract had already expired, this opened the door for our client to negotiate each item one at a time.

A month later, the suppliers expressed their exhaustion with the deal. This combined with their vision of securing such a large contract made the difference. Since they were a publicly traded company, they said the sales forecasts were already accounted for in their earnings estimate. Their profit margins will still be good enough at the lower price. Additionally, selling such a large amount of product over a five-year term provided the long-term production security their president and board needed. We uncovered their need for the agreement. The relationship is still intact because our clients were respectful and openly shared the data supporting a price decrease. The new contract, close to their "optimal" pricing, saved our clients approximately five hundred thousand per year. The supplier said no twice, and the negotiation still resulted in a great conclusion for our client. Although our client became uncomfortable watching the timeline for the deal extend, the supplier experienced the same uncertainty. Time can work in your favor if you have patience.

When you find yourself leading a protracted negotiation, keeping your team calm isn't easy. The concept of seeking decisions in each phase of the deal, especially giving your opponent the right to say no, becomes more difficult the longer the negotiation process extends. The more consequential the decisions, the more emotions will come into play. If you're not careful, when you allocate more time, energy, money, and emotion to reaching an agreement, your need for the deal will naturally increase. The temptation to bargain for the sake of saving time can be expensive. If you find yourself getting fatigued, take a break and regroup. When you experience this pressure, systematic preparation helps you focus. Instead of agonizing over what's at stake, determine the decisions that keep you from giving up too much too soon.

Another challenge we face with coaching is when the leader drives groupthink within their team. Even if a leader has a tight connection with their team, dominating the group can lead to a weakened agreement. Opposing views are not a bad thing. If you're the boss, and you're closed off to healthy pushback, don't be surprised when you find yourself on your own. A leader pushing too hard to gain consensus on their personal views of the decisions at hand is wasting time. What's worse, they're missing out on valuable contributions.

Reaching alignment internally can be tenuous. Avoid showing your frustration. Always remain nurturing and respectful of your team's perspectives. Leadership negotiations are challenging because you might be tempted to exert your authority and tell people, "You'll agree to this or else."

I know identifying decisions you want may seem obvious. You probably think hearing the word "yes" repeatedly from your team means they support your decision. Be careful when you see heads nodding in approval. Do they really agree with what you're saying, or are they afraid to speak up?

VISION DRIVES DECISION

Vision drives decisions, and reaching agreements require numerous decisions. If our clients routinely ask themselves, "What does the opposition see in this deal?" this habit alone will improve their success dramatically. The biggest challenge for everyone is remaining patient enough to build and uncover vision.

Realistically, keeping track of all agreements a leader is engaged with and taking the time to build a checklist to prepare for each event isn't feasible. On the other hand, by committing the key steps in our negotiation checklist to memory, the effort to reach important agreements becomes easier and more effective.

The process of preparing for a negotiation can become second nature with practice. The decisions you want is a key step. A "no" along the way does not mean you're losing the deal. A "no" from your team doesn't mean they've lost trust. The opposite is true. Telling a negotiation opponent no respectfully will not damage the relationship. Remember, strong and enduring deals don't come easy.

In the next chapter, I'll help you determine why someone's not saying yes. Once you can determine what's behind your opponent's decisions, we'll examine our final checklist step, "What Happens Next."

CHAPTER 8:

THE FOUR REASONS PEOPLE SAY NO—A CASE STUDY

The title of my father's book, *Start with No*, implies decisions determine our direction in a negotiation. In the leadership arena, they'll also be your measurement for what it takes to solidify an agreement and establish alignment with your team.

Mission and purpose, problems, and identifying decisions you want helps you prepare to execute the negotiation. The fourth step, "What Happens Next," is more of an "in the moment" reaction. This step is predicated on what you learn during the event.

The vision of your opponent, new problems, decisions, indecision, who, and how decisions are reached will guide you from start to finish. Although you can prepare and anticipate what happens next, let's pause here and examine the four reasons why people say no.

During my absence from Camp Negotiations, my brother, Todd Camp, with help from our coaching team and countless coaching client interactions, had quantified these four reasons. According to Todd, any decision short of a "yes," like a "no," "let me think it over," or "maybe," falls into at least one of four categories.

In a recent interview with Todd, he said:

> Just as clients form the habit of building a checklist, they begin to see decisions as benchmarks for where they stand and where they should shift their focus. The toughest part of coaching is making sure the client understands that decisions are not final, they can always be changed. By not assuming what decisions will be made and managing expectations, when our clients hear no they are prepared to prosecute the list in a much calmer manner. We also tell our clients to treat a "maybe" as a "no." The lack of a clear decision from the other is dangerous. There's a reason they're not ready to agree or disagree. Looking at the four reasons is helpful in these situations.

REASON 1: MISSING THE EMOTIONAL VISION OF BENEFIT—THEY DON'T SEE IT

The first reason why people say no is the one we encounter most often. Jim Sr. would use the word "pain" and encourage his clients to focus on the vision of their opponent. "Pain" refers to the big challenge your client is trying to overcome. The importance for you to provide a clear vision of solutions cannot be overstated. If your opponent can embrace your mission and purpose, which is purely focused to their benefit, the easier it will become for them to act.

The more clearly your opponent can define what they need to solve, and the easier they can visualize how you can help them, the closer they'll be to an agreement. If those you're negotiating with don't see the vision of benefit, or they can't attach emotionally to finding a solution to a problem, they won't say yes to what you're proposing. Whenever you hit a roadblock in any agreement, your focal point is what the other side sees.

How are they emotionally connected to the decision? Your ideas won't matter if they can't "see" how they benefit.[1]

REASON 2: LACK OF SUPPORTING DATA

The second reason people say no is due to a lack of supporting data. You may have a product or solution where the information you're sharing makes perfect sense to you. You might ask, "Why can't they see this? This is simple." Maybe your idea sounds too good? Although what you're offering can solve a problem, simply making guarantees without information to back it up can prevent someone from saying yes.

Have you bought something thinking, *This is a no-brainer?* You initially get excited and think, *Yes, I need this.* Still, in the back of your mind, you're struggling. *Can it be this simple? Can this really help me?* Even if your purchase seemed like a perfect opportunity to fill a need, you say to yourself, *This is too easy. What am I missing? Where's the data? Where's the proof this is a good deal?*

If you're a leader you might be tempted to mandate a solution. You may not have time to provide supporting data, or it may even seem ridiculous to imagine any data is required for those expected to follow your direction. Once you establish a clear vision of "why" what you're seeking is important, have the patience to provide what they need to verify your ideas. This reinforces their decision to follow you. If you're a leader without data to support what you're asking, don't fake it. If what you want someone to agree to is based on anecdotal evidence, tell the truth, and take responsibility if you're wrong. If you're seeking decisions where everyone's taking a risk, put your lack of evidence up front. This situation is a great example of a problem to address in your checklist.

REASON 3: DON'T HAVE THE AUTHORITY TO SAY YES
Perhaps the people you're talking to lack the authority to say yes. A good example of this dynamic is seen when we're coaching companies securing supply chain agreements. Suppliers offering products, materials, or services often find themselves under extreme pricing pressure. The procurement teams they negotiate with are savvy when it comes to reducing the costs. Our clients hear statements like, "Your pricing is too high. If you can't provide a discount, we'll have to go another direction and remove you from the bidding process."

When coaching these clients, we've discovered procurement professionals may not have the ultimate power to make a final decision. They've been trained and tasked by their leadership to lower costs. Unfortunately, they'll go to extremes and suggest the supplier is damaging the business relationship by asking for such a high price. Please don't misunderstand me, we don't dislike purchasing. We also coach procurement teams. What I'm suggesting is the person you're working with may not be authorized to make the final decision on their own. When our clients hold firm on price, the decision is typically elevated within the buyer's company. Maybe there are more layers to decisions than we initially assumed.

If you're a leader trying to reach an internal agreement, keep in mind where decisions are ultimately reached. Who has the final say? Who should be included in the decision process you're overlooking? People find it easier to say no when they don't have the power to say yes.

REASON 4: THE BLUFF

Bluffing is the fourth reason people say no. They might tell you no to push you into a compromise or to see how you react. They might be hoping you'll lower your price or change your terms. Rejecting your final proposal might be a tactic to see if you're willing to sweeten the deal. We see this all the time. You might think you're missing the mark completely when you hear the word "no." Instead, you could be closer to an agreement than you think. In our system we encourage our clients to prepare for and be willing to hear the word "no" multiple times. The key is not to panic.

In leadership, your team may initially reject the decisions you want because it means too much work for them to execute your plan. They may be testing your conviction. Your reaction to their displeasure is critical. If you start to waver or display frustration, they'll continue to push back. This is where you relax and stick to your checklist. People can't bluff indefinitely.

Keeping these four reasons in mind will help you discover why your opponent is rejecting. Don't assume you need to present more information. Don't search for data arbitrarily hoping it will make a difference. Make sure you understand their decision-making process and who is involved. Most importantly, don't give up when you hear the word "no." Each time, rather than trying to *push* to a yes, stay in your opponent's world and patiently *pull* them back to the pain or vision you've already uncovered.

CASE STUDY EXAMPLE OF THE PRINCIPLES IN ACTION

I've provided a personal experience below to hopefully demonstrate these principles. I didn't plan on initiating this negotiation, nor did I anticipate getting involved given my rank and position. This deal turned out to have significant strategic implications for the military and gave me an opportunity to apply our system to a problem I deeply wanted to solve.

In the military aviation community, it takes years to become good at your job. Training is a continuous requirement, even for those flying for decades. Each aircraft has a unique list of maneuvers and training events. Aviators need to constantly demonstrate their proficiency. In 2013, I signed up for a routine training mission. This would be one of my last flights in the KC-135R air refueler before being reassigned to state headquarters. My student was a young copilot in the process of upgrading to become an aircraft commander. A normal day at the office for an instructor pilot involved this type of training mission. With thousands of hours in the tanker, my role included oversight while he practiced takeoffs and landings on a windy day, where the winds were close to being out of safe limits. Flying in strong crosswinds is a great way to verify a pilot's abilities. If he did well, his next flight would be a certification flight, his "check ride."

On the first approach for a touch-and-go landing, I had no issues with his technique. He handled the crosswinds perfectly. Approaching the touchdown point, the jet gently settled on the runway. He made the same mistake I'd seen many times in my career. Instead of holding the flight control inputs to keep the airplane in the middle of the runway, I heard a long exhale over his microphone. Still holding my breath, I stayed alert during this dangerous point in the landing. He instantly relaxed his control inputs while pushing up the throttles to gain speed for takeoff. Instinctively, I took physical control of the airplane and said, "I've got the aircraft." Military pilots are trained to expect this. The instructor takes over, providing corrective action to avoid an accident.

When he relaxed the controls, the aircraft started drifting to the edge of the runway. A couple of more feet and a half of a second later, we could have departed the runway. The results would have been catastrophic. During the mission debrief, a good friend and highly experienced pilot in the jump seat verified my need to react quickly. He and the student were happy I intervened.

Three years later, I found myself telling this story to a group of personnel leaders in Washington, DC. In my new personnel role, I found myself negotiating on behalf of all flying wings and full-time instructor pilots in the Air National Guard.

During my second year at headquarters, they promoted me to colonel and put me in charge of human resources. Our team of forty supported numerous air and army units. We serviced seventeen thousand soldiers, airmen, and civilians serving in a military, federal, and state capacity. With a broad scope of work, we struggled to keep up. On a normal day we received hundreds of emails and constant calls from commanders in the field. I must admit, I missed flying and couldn't wait to get a command assignment putting me back into an airplane.

During a quarterly meeting with the wing commanders and senior leadership staff, the commander of my previous tanker unit expressed serious concerns over how many of his full-time instructor pilots recently resigned. They were leaving for a higher paying career in the airlines. The two-star general in command at the time didn't seem too alarmed. I remember him saying, "We've seen this before.

This is a normal cycle. Pilot demand ebbs and flows in the airline business." In the Air National Guard, the majority of our full-time instructor pilots were federal employees who were also serving in the military. Unlike active-duty Air Force offering large bonuses to retain pilots, the federal system lacked the funding to take the same measures. Although most of our pilots heading to commercial aviation would remain in the unit and serve part-time, replacing someone with years of instructor experience is not easy. In the KC-135, for example, from start to finish it normally took six to seven years to grow an instructor pilot from scratch.

At the conclusion of our meeting, other commanders expressed with me privately their pilot attrition worries. Being one of the only instructors and former airline pilot in the country serving in a personnel officer position, this gave me a unique perspective on the growing problem. I did the same thing in 1997, leaving a full-time instructor position, after only two years, for a job at United Airlines. The next day, I asked a young army captain to pull the data for our instructor pilot vacancies in Ohio and the national level, if possible. He informed me the full-time personnel system indicated normal pilot levels in Ohio. He also shared he didn't have access to the nationwide numbers. Nationally, the Air National Guard employs over one thousand full-time instructor pilots serving in dozens of Air Force units. With the air national guard flying most of the aircraft in the Air Force inventory, losing too many experienced pilots would take years to replace. The initial data didn't make sense to me. Why were the commanders concerned if most of the positions were occupied? What were we missing?

I asked our team to take a closer look at our recent attrition. We discovered our pilots leaving were in the middle of their twenty- to twenty-five-year career. Compensation in the federal pay system is based on position, grade, and longevity. For example, a new hire who's not finished with instructor training would be a GS-12 or GS-13 pay level with less than a few years in service. They would likely be a step one to three on the wage table. Conversely, a senior level instructor pilot would be a step eight to ten level and have close to twenty years or more of experience. A bell curve of the pilot workforce should reflect most being in the middle of the pay scale, or approximately midway through their career.

The initial data in Ohio didn't validate my concerns. Our pilot positions were filled; however, we verified a big tenure gap in the middle. With most of our senior instructors close to retirement and little experience behind them, we could be heading for a major safety issue in Ohio. Many new full-time pilots were quietly building their flight hours until they could get picked up by a major airline. Most would not be in the seat long enough to even become an instructor, let alone have enough experience to take the controls from a student in a dangerous scenario. Did we have an acute problem in Ohio or were we on the cusp of discovering a broader issue?

In order to validate the situation at the national level, I reached out to the National Guard Bureau asking for help. I wanted the demographics of the entire pilot force. Surprisingly, they denied me access. They said I had no authority to make such a big request. I heard my first no in what would unfold into a long and tenuous negotiation. Sitting in my office with my young team, we discussed options. Without the national data, we would have little chance of even quantifying the problem, let alone trying to identify a solution. I'd hopefully return to flying and might even get the chance to command a unit someday. Therefore, I couldn't ignore this problem. Digging deeper and researching the airline industry, the outlook didn't look good. The airlines couldn't hire fast enough to keep up with industry growth and pilot retirements. Hiring projections revealed this would only get worse over time.

Reporting to my boss, the adjutant general for Ohio, I knew my first negotiation would be with him. I had to help him see and discover my mission and purpose. I wanted him to ultimately turn me loose on this problem. During our first meeting on this subject, I shared with him my M&P: "By accessing and analyzing the national instructor pilot data, we could address a serious degradation in pilot experience levels. This would ultimately preserve operational war time capabilities and ensure safe training operations in the future."

Thankfully, he approved my plan to go after the data. He supported me and agreed to weigh-in and help when needed. He knew I would run into issues dealing with high-ranking generals at the national level. Neither of us expected they would completely shut me down at the national level. I couldn't even get a return phone call. Don't get me wrong, these folks are great patriots and hard workers. My frustration didn't stop me from trying to get the ear of someone who would listen.

Getting no response, probably due to my rank, they clearly lacked the *vision*, *data*, and perhaps the *authority* to acknowledge the problem in the first place. I was compelled to keep going until I could call their *bluff*. The same is true when trying to start a negotiation with any large or complex organization. Finding the right people to engage with, the actual decision makers, is the biggest challenge.

For weeks I made numerous phone calls attempting to find a point of contact. My team and I sent multiple emails and got no response. When I finally reached a retired army colonel by phone, who's now a civilian working for the national guard's federal employee program, he denied my request to meet with him in DC. He reiterated we were not authorized to examine the national data. Furthermore, he said their system showed most of the positions were filled. He didn't see the problem. When I ended the call by asking, "Where do I go from here?" he said, "This is way above my paygrade, and you probably need to engage with the major general in charge of the national guard personnel. I'm not sure how you can solve the data problem. Without it, you won't get an audience."

Unfortunately, I still couldn't access the information through his directorate. I needed more than an anecdotal argument to get the right level of attention. Without asking for permission, I connected with other human resource directors in different states. Having met many of them at military conferences, I hoped they would share the same information we'd pieced together in Ohio. During the calls, I shared my M&P, clearly defined the potential problem, and asked for their help. Many rejected my request because policy prohibited sharing this kind of information. For the handful agreeing to work with me, I assured them I would accept the risk and take responsibility for negative fallout. I also promised to confidentially share my collective data. Thankfully, they offered enough support for me to make a case.

With the pilot data compiled from eleven other states, we created a visual presentation of the problem. Instead of a healthy bell curve of experience, with most of our instructor pilots in the midpoint of their career, the middle didn't exist. This frightened me. I had to keep going. Instead of emailing the information and potentially creating objections with those who could get the information in front of the decision makers in Washington, DC, I hopped on a flight to meet with the personnel section in the Air National Guard Readiness Center.

Fortunately, the brigadier general running the directorate flew C-130s in his previous assignment in the Air Guard. He agreed with my assessment and assigned a colonel with an extensive personnel background to assist. She knew most of the players in the National Guard Bureau, and I welcomed her help. The general also cautioned me, saying the federal employment branch is too busy and probably wouldn't allocate anyone on their staff to look at the pilot issue. He smiled and said, "They already think pilots are overpaid. Good luck, Jim." His comment verified what I had already suspected: Most of their personnel team had emotional baggage over Air Force pilots in general.

During our first in-person meeting, the retired army colonel hit us with more bad news. Regardless of what our information suggested, the pay scales are determined by the Office of Personnel Management. To make matters worse, a separate budget didn't exist for pilot retention incentives. The funds would have to come from the National Guard's federal employee account. Although an incentive program existed in the past, they discontinued the program many years prior due to improper usage in other National Guard career fields. The regulations also stated a federal employee would have to have another job offer in hand or be in jeopardy of leaving federal service before a financial incentive could be offered. He sympathized with our challenge and said we were facing an uphill battle with little chance of success.

I knew when an airline presented one of our pilots with a job offer, it would be too late. The hiring process in the airline business is extensive. Filling out the application alone and preparing for an interview is a major commitment. Once a pilot starts down this road, they rarely turn back. When I headed back to Ohio with another "no" in hand, I set another meeting with my boss. We needed to get the actual numbers of those "considering" leaving for the airlines. No database could answer this question. Commanders across the country would have to have difficult discussions with their instructor pilots. They'd have to ask the question most would hesitate to answer. Even our commanders in Ohio expressed discomfort having this conversation with their pilots. No one wanted to say, "Yes, boss, I'm planning to leave and go to the airlines."

A major benchmark for eligibility for an airline job is qualifying for an airline transport pilot (ATP) certificate. This requires 1,500 flight hours and passing a Federal Aviation Administration check ride. In addition to accumulating the flight hours, a military pilot would have to invest thousands of dollars to take the civilian exam. With the support of my boss, I released a white paper across the country soliciting commanders to identify how many of their full-time instructor pilots met these experience qualifications. I also attended a few commander conferences to socialize the problem and ask for support. When the army major general in charge of all personnel in the Army and Air National Guard had the chance to read the white paper, he tasked his federal team to take a closer look into our problem. He wanted a follow-up meeting with his team if they concurred with the problem, data, and potential courses of action.

When we met with the general's federal team, they finally acknowledged the scope of our problem. When I asked the question, "What happens next?" they stared at me with a puzzled look on their faces. I quickly followed up with another question: "What can we do to restart the federal incentive program?" We knew it would take years for the Office of Personnel Management to program for additional funding. The personnel team replied telling us we would have to submit incentive request packages one pilot at a time. When I asked, "What concerns do you have with this process?" they responded with apprehension and said each request would be time consuming and heavily scrutinized.

Their team accepted when I offered our workforce from Ohio to assist in completing the packages. One month later, and after numerous failed attempts to get an incentive approved, four pilots in Ohio were approved for a 25 percent pay incentive. The funds would come from the unit's internal budget. Our commander in Ohio happily agreed to earmark money from his unit's internal account. He couldn't afford to lose another instructor. All four pilots took the deal. They agreed to stay full-time, and the news traveled fast. Within days, commanders from units across the country asked for our help. We cracked the code. Over the next few months, the personnel folks in DC were inundated with pilot incentive requests.

Pilots nationwide were rethinking the idea of leaving for airline jobs. The younger pilots were optimistic the pay scale would eventually reflect parity with active-duty pilots' compensation. In 2017, after dozens of incentive packages were approved, the Office of Personnel Management enacted a substantial pay increase for pilots across the board.

Who knows how many accidents we avoided by retaining our experienced aviators? I've shortened the summary of this negotiation for good reason. This negotiation lasted for close to two years in total. I'll admit, I enjoyed this one. This had a huge impact on our military and our small HR team in Ohio. Once the federal team in DC engaged, they were amazing in their resolve. Our mission and purpose, and the vision we created, drove the decisions. Today, the incentive process has spread to other career fields in the Army and Air National Guard, and the Office of Personnel Management is in the process of adjusting outdated pay scales. Luckily, one of those first four pilots we incentivized to stay recently replaced me. He is the new commander in Ohio and will promote to major general soon.

Whether you're working on a strategic negotiation like the one I've shared or dealing with one person trying to reach a simple agreement, decisions are everything. Hopefully you see a combination of the four reasons people say no can coexist. When I first brought the pilot problem to light, not knowing who to engage, I found myself surrounded by barriers. I had a *vision* others couldn't see. Concerned with experience and continuing to fly airplanes safely, I still couldn't pinpoint the *data* suggesting a problem even existed. The first people I engaged lacked the *authority* to make changes. Many gave me a quick "no" simply to resist change. Perhaps their *bluff* tested my commitment? Either way, when you prosecute the four reasons why people say no, figuring out your next step, "What Happens Next," will keep your negotiation moving. Even if you don't see instant progress, a system gives you more control when you hit a wall and get frustrated trying to reach a deal.

CHAPTER 9

CHECKLIST STEP 4: WHAT HAPPENS NEXT

The final step in our system is identifying what happens next. In this step, you set the agenda for the next phase. These are your future actions where you seek agreement on the follow-on steps for both sides. Like a game plan in athletics, negotiation success is predicated on how you react and adjust to your opponent. Although predicting your counterpart's decision-making and behaviors is impossible, preparing for what happens, post decisions, will help you stay focused and in control of your emotions. If you're negotiating an agreement where you anticipate multiple engagements, this step will help you address all forms of communication in the deal, including your response to an email.

Reaching a tentative deal without the next steps being clearly defined and agreed to can be in jeopardy of falling apart. Even if you think the negotiation is moving in your favor, omitting this step can lead to misunderstanding. Whether you're working on an internal one-on-one meeting, or a complex business deal, this is your follow through. This is your chance to clarify and set expectations. Preparing for your next move is a must. Let's examine a few scenarios to reinforce the importance of establishing your next steps.

WHAT HAPPENS WHEN PEOPLE CAN'T DECIDE

When you discover someone's unable to decide, don't be surprised or discouraged. Be aware, if you rush decisions, they can backfire. People's emotions take over when pushed. The moment you apply too much pressure, you'll come across aggressive and needy. Whoever you're trying to reach an agreement with, this alone can cloud the vision you've worked hard to build. Remember, you cannot control the decision-making of others. The safest way to deal with indecision is to treat a "maybe" like a "no."

In 2022, at one of our large bases in Ohio, we found ourselves unexpectedly searching for a new commander. The sitting boss unexpectedly needed to retire well before we anticipated. Looking across our bench of eligible colonels, one looked like a perfect fit. With years of experience in the unit's mission and service in all the requisite leadership positions, he seemed like a logical choice. We recently promoted him to deputy base commander and assumed he would jump at the opportunity to lead his unit. With only a few months to get him ready, I asked him for an in-person meeting.

During our visit I asked, "What are your thoughts of being the next commander?" I assumed this would excite him and he'd quickly say yes. Instead, he mentioned his eligibility for a full military retirement in less than a year. His expression and body language signaled his uneasiness. While continuing to discuss the needs of the base, I could sense he became overwhelmed. Although I wanted to solve this problem quickly, I knew he wasn't ready to decide. I reassured him we had time for him to consider the job and emphasized he could tell me no. After a brief silence, he asked, "What happens if I turn down the job today?"

I gave him an honest answer. I told him I'd start exploring other options. He understood my predicament and respectfully told me no. He relaxed when I again reinforced it was okay. I shook his hand and thanked him for his honesty and decisiveness. I also mentioned how much I appreciated his continued leadership.

We continued discussing the challenges facing his unit, and he asked if he could have time to process the opportunity for command. When I suggested we might have to advertise the position nationwide, he expressed concerns with bringing in a commander from another state. He said this would not sit well with his airmen. Sympathetic to his concern, I stressed we couldn't afford to rely on a "possible" replacement. He agreed with my sense of urgency. I had no choice and needed to start a wide search.

Walking out of the office, I asked him why he declined. He openly revealed he didn't see himself being considered for the opportunity. He continued by saying his family was already excited for his retirement. He knew the job would mean staying in uniform for an additional two years. Rather than push him into saying yes, I helped him say no. I hoped his emotions would level out helping him logically process this opportunity. I didn't like the idea of needing to convince anyone to accept an opportunity for command. What happened next is exactly what I wanted.

A couple of days later at our quarterly leadership meeting, he approached with a big smile. He thanked me for my patience and laughed. He told me rejecting command upset his wife. She said, "Why didn't you tell the general yes?" Although they were planning on retirement, their family reconsidered and offered their support.

He did a great job in command and enjoyed his experience. Coincidentally, he and I retired within a couple of months of each other. After my retirement ceremony, he walked up and thanked me for allowing him to change his mind. He said allowing him to say no and giving his family time to discuss the decision made all the difference.

I know it might seem counterproductive to move from a "maybe" to a "no." Whenever you encounter someone who's unable to decide, and if time permits, giving them space to think is a natural next step. When they say no, their emotions lower, giving them time to use intellect and logic.

The problem with getting stuck on a "maybe" is people rarely move to a decision on their own. In addition to concealing your need for the decision you want, at least a "no" gives you time to address objections. If you can't overcome what's holding them back from a "yes," at least you can adjust your course and avoid wasting your time chasing a "maybe."[1] Negotiators allowing someone to say no have a better chance of eventually hearing yes. In this case, "what happens next" keeps the door open for further dialogue and another decision.

SLOW DOWN—YOU DON'T HAVE A DEAL

Ironically, when you're sensing the negotiation is moving in a positive direction, skipping this step can make you vulnerable to assumptions and false expectations. You might be thinking, *What a great meeting. Looks like we're close to a deal.* Our client's excitement in the moment interferes with their focus, and they forget this step altogether.

When you're excited, keep in mind negotiations are ongoing. We tell our coaching clients they don't have a deal until both sides deliver what they agreed upon. When you hear the word "yes," have the patience to focus on the next steps. Details can resurface and sabotage your agreement if avoided. Unaddressed problems or unanticipated change of decisions after the fact could lead to you to renegotiating previous agreements.

Dave DeSantis, my coaching partner, and I recently worked with a commercial sales team in the Midwest. Their company manufactured and installed large vehicle maintenance facilities across the country. During our negotiation debrief with our client, he happily shared his customer agreed to expand from one facility on the East Coast to two additional locations. He said the pricing and terms in his proposal were acceptable to his client. When I asked him, "What's your next step? What happens next?" he paused. He said, "I'm not sure on the exact timing for the next two installs, and they emailed me this morning asking our engineers to put together a quote for five more locations."

Our coaching client's excitement distracted him from following his checklist. I suggested he reply to his customer's email with the following:

> Hi, John. Thank you for the call yesterday. We're happy to start working on the additional locations once we clarify our next steps on the three designs we provided last month. Before I process the purchase order for these locations we discussed, what does your timing look like for payment and installation?

Before he sent the email, we discussed the possibility of his client asking for a discount if they expanded the size of the deal. Putting together designs for the additional five locations would tie up him and his team for a month. I stressed he should nail down the first deal before tying up his resources for a future agreement. He agreed with me, saying he got ahead of himself when he read the customer's email. He's now progressing on the first two locations. Our client admitted finalizing the terms of the first deal was going to require more decisions and take much longer than expected. Two months into coaching him on this deal, he found even more problems if they expand to the next five locations. He planned to slow down and ensure what happens next was clarified after each interaction with his customer.

YOU HAVE A "NO." WHAT'S NEXT?

Another possibility in the heat of a deal is you hear the word "no," or you find yourself saying, "No." This is not necessarily the end of the negotiation. Hopefully, when you've prepared, this is something you're ready to hear and willing to say. If you've openly given the right to veto, and if you've maintained a respectful posture, this is your chance to uncover the real problems.

Jim Camp Sr. believed the negotiation ends when you decide. You're in control. A "no" is only a decision and doesn't imply the deal is off. Don't be afraid of this. Stay focused on your opponent's pain or vision. This will uncover the real problems and give you a better understanding of their decision. Identifying what happens next helps you to keep going. You decide the level of effort you're willing to devote to reach an agreement.[2]

Based on the four reasons people say no discussed in the previous chapter, what happens next is the chance for you to explore what's behind a decision. For example, the next time you hit resistance in a deal, try asking questions like, "Where are we falling short?" "What problems have we overlooked?" "How did you arrive at your decision?" "Where should we go from here?" If you're still unsure how to continue in the negotiation, or you're struggling to find a good question, try asking verbatim, "What happens next?"

YOUR TEAM'S WATCHING WHAT YOU DO NEXT

No matter how much you prepare, not all agreements are going to go your way. Whether you're facing a personal disappointment, or your team experiences a big setback during a business deal, "What happens next?" is also a reminder. People watch their leadership. Your response and persistence can inspire your teammates.

Most of you reading this have experienced rejection after a job interview. Personally, I've been told no many times. In fact, I've been rejected three times trying to become a commander. When you're turned down in front of your peers, this is a great opportunity to show your resilience. I've shared with many airmen my perspective on being told no. My advice is always the same: "When you hear no to any opportunity, what happens next will define you." Keep your poise and control your emotions. Everyone's watching your actions and behavior. Because you were denied a job after the interview doesn't mean the end of the road. Decisions can change late in the hiring process, or you might be a good fit in another role.

In business negotiations, this is also the case. How a leader responds to adversity and uncertainty impacts your team. According to my brother and business partner, Todd Camp:

The start-up CEO often struggles when they don't have much capital remaining, yet they see a potential exit on the horizon. These folks are all intelligent, if not brilliant. However, they may not have experience in holding a team together under extreme pressure. It's great to watch them become comfortable being uncomfortable. When they approach all these important negotiations using a system, you can see their teams building trust with each other. If the leader can stay strong in these difficult environments, the team sees that confidence and rally behind them.

Let your team watch you dig into what happens next, and your leader-follower agreement will strengthen. I've experienced numerous negotiations where I knew I'd be told no. At times my peers would question me, "Why would you attempt to influence changes when the obstacles looked too big to overcome?" If you're leading people, remember: They don't have a permanent obligation to follow you. They will if your actions inspire them.

According to Ohio's State Command Chief Master Sergeant Troy Taylor, "Having the courage to run into a wall for your people is one thing, but a leader willing to bounce off the wall and keep going is huge. When they see you're willing to fight on their behalf, they'll follow you to the end of the earth."

My willingness to pursue a seemingly impossible negotiation is always motivated by my mission and purpose. Hearing the word "no" is not a failure. Instead, you can show your team your wiliness to pursue agreements on their behalf.

For my entire military career, I can recall most of my fellow airmen being frustrated with the Air Force fitness test. The need to be in shape is not the issue. We questioned the validity of the test itself. I couldn't have imagined we would have the chance to influence this policy. From our level, changing the way the Air Force measured our fitness seemed non-negotiable.

Maintaining physical fitness standards in the military is a reality for everyone in uniform. Depending on the branch of service, tests are administered to ensure members stay in shape. The Air Force mantra is airmen must be "fit to fight." Outside temporary exemptions from the fitness test like medical or other administrative waivers, this is a yearly requirement. Unfortunately, we faced too many discharges due to poor performance on the test.

In 2016, a squadron commander and his senior enlisted leader asked me to meet with a young lady on the verge of being kicked out for failing her test. Only three years into her six-year enlistment, and halfway complete with her college degree, if discharged she would lose her tuition support. What was even worse was she loved serving her country and looked forward to her first deployment. Her squadron leadership asked me to reconsider discharge, saying she had a great attitude and is close to passing her test. They further explained she recently passed a practice test getting ready for the real thing. This upset me because a previous Air Force policy allowed airmen to test early. If an airmen received a passing score before their due month, the score would count, and they were compliant for another year. Being aware of the policy change, I disagreed with the rationale: Apparently, taking the test too often increased the workload for those administering the test.

When I asked her what happened on her final test, she admitted her nerves disrupted her sleep the night before. She also admitted being intimidated by the testing team, telling me she threw up in the restroom moments before the running portion of the test. This young lady did not compete athletically in high school or college, and she struggled since basic training to stay in shape. Since roughly 40 percent of the score was based on the circumference of her abdomen, her natural body composition also made it difficult for her to pass.

Although I offered her an exception to the policy to retake the test, a week later she declined my offer. She said she didn't want to struggle any longer. She received an honorable discharge. This did not sit well with me. This problem is a recurring one throughout the Air Force. At the time, I wasn't focused on the hundreds of thousands of personnel in the Air Force. Still, it deeply concerned me for the rest of my teammates under my command.

After consulting with our base legal team, searching for ways to improve the overall physical fitness of our members, they cautioned me against superseding Air Force policy. Shortly after hearing a "no" from my legal advisors, I continued to research the problem. I discovered this is a systemic issue across the country. The abdominal circumference measurement had a maximum limit regardless of how strong or how fast someone could run. Therefore, if you're naturally thin you have a distinct advantage. If you were six-five and played offensive guard for the Air Force Academy like a pilot in my former tanker unit, passing the waist measurement would be a constant struggle. Luckily, he ran fast enough to make up the difference.

Airmen going on crash diets before the test also became a disturbing trend. I'm all for standards and accountability, except we were losing good people not for a lack of effort. I believed the test and the performance standards were flawed. For example, a thirty- to thirty-nine-year-old male or female had to hit the same level of performance. Last time I checked in any sport, a ten-year span can create a huge difference for any athlete.

Shortly after I decided to pursue this negotiation with Air Force headquarters, I met with our senior staff members and asked for their support. They all knew my proposed negotiation would be over before it even started. Regardless, I wanted to start by making internal changes to our testing process. Surprisingly, they were mostly in agreement with the idea. We had a valid mission and purpose, and the problems in our control were manageable. My first move would be starting the negotiation with our airmen.

I wanted all of them to decide. Either reject or accept changing the way we approached the test. Rather than waiting until the last minute to prepare for the test, we would keep track of everyone's fitness efforts. I made "what happens next" clear to our people regardless of their initial buy-in. If any airman put forth the effort and tested on time, I would do everything in my power to prevent demotions and discharges if they fell short. On a case-by-case basis, I had the command authority to determine legal disposition.

I'll admit, at first many rejected the idea. I knew they would tell me no regardless of my desire to help them succeed. I started reinforcing my new agenda by saying, "We will offer an official or a practice test anytime you're ready. Preparing for the test is in your control, and failing to pass the test is not a bad thing. If you test on time and can demonstrate you're making the effort to improve, I'll fight for you." I also made another promise to my entire team. I told them I'd do everything in my power to change the Air Force's testing policy.

Everyone understood the first step was cleaning up our own fitness issues. This would help us set an example the Air Force couldn't ignore. Our team quietly initiated a negotiation to change the Air Force fitness test all knowing headquarters would tell us no. We expected this. Once they all realized my commitment to getting the policy changed for the good of all airmen, they all agreed to "what happens next." We would provide data and create a vision at the national level. Over the next year, we had no late tests and no fitness discharges at the 179th Airlift Wing. Everyone in the wing embraced the agreement. Squadrons were practicing the fitness test, and the fitness culture on the base started changing for the better.

After being reassigned to state headquarters overseeing each unit in the state, I made sure to spread word across the entire Air National Guard: "Ohio is attempting to change the fitness test." I expanded what we started in Mansfield by negotiating internally with our own leadership teams across the state. Although I was in command, instead of demanding compliance, I followed my negotiation checklist.

Many were skeptical we could influence change in the Air Force. Still, they all agreed to help us gather the data. We started keeping track, compiling the practice testing scores across all five thousand Ohio airmen. Our practice scores and official testing results improved significantly.

When I attempted to get an exception to policy allowing for practice tests, the National Guard bureau told me no. When I inquired to understand their vision behind their decision, I received a phone call from the head of Air National Guard personnel. She stated they could do nothing in Washington to help me. I then asked the general, "Where do I go from here? What happens next?" In confidence, she told me to ask support from my adjutant general to create our own Ohio Air National Guard fitness policy.

Even though we were a component of the Air Force, we could take the risk in Ohio by adapting our own policy. If we adhered to the same performance standards and didn't change the test itself, we had the latitude to administer the test on our terms. Although she didn't have the authority to tell me yes, she pointed out a legal opportunity.

The adjutant general reports first to the governor and has authority over airmen serving in a state status. Therefore, we legally adapted a temporary policy for the purpose of conducting a study, one which helped the Air Force and the airmen in Ohio. This is exactly what I needed to reach internal alignment with our commanders in the field. The entire state jumped on board.

For the next few years, the Ohio Air National Guard continued to refine and improve our fitness testing policy. In addition to allowing early testing, we separated the abdominal measurement and the physical portions of the test. This ensured airmen were properly nourished and hydrated prior to the athletic testing events. The results were staggering. Luckily, my wing command replacement at Mansfield, now a brigadier general and director of operations for the entire Air National Guard, had the ear of many senior leaders in Washington, DC. She helped the negotiation by encouraging these leaders to look at our data. In 2021, the Air Force changed their fitness test.[3] Their final solution closely mirrored our policy in Ohio.

Although the Air Force did not publicly acknowledge Ohio, we received word from various insiders that our data made a big difference. When the negotiation seemed to end with "no," defining what happened next helped fulfill my mission and purpose for the airmen.

Looking back over numerous business negotiations, even when our clients thought they reached a final "no," the deal didn't end. I know identifying what happens next at the end of a failed agreement might seem pointless, but we've seen the opposite. Setting an agenda with the opposition, allowing them to reengage if their situation changes, often leads to deals reigniting. Demonstrating the willingness to hear a "no" and not wavering on your terms can be enough to keep the door open for continued negotiations.

Determining what happens next and holding to your agreed upon expectations is critical to maintaining the trust of your team. When you demonstrate patience and the willingness to listen, act decisively, and consistently follow through, you're mirroring the behaviors of an effective negotiator. Holding firm to your acceptable terms and avoiding the temptation to compromise also demonstrates sincerity with your business opponent.

Your persistence after hearing the word "no" and transitioning to "what happens next" leads to success. You'll find the subject, setting, and the scope of the desired agreement doesn't matter. By now, you should see the relationship between leading and negotiating. Trust, dependability, and resiliency are critical to both.

CHAPTER 10

NEGOTIATION LOG— WHAT JUST HAPPENED

While coaching negotiations, we often find ourselves dropped into the middle of a complex deal. Helping the individual or team develop a negotiation log is our first step. Unless the situation requires an urgent response, we insist on a systematic breakdown of what's already occurred. This gives our client the chance to share their perspectives on where the agreement currently stands. Our log only consists of three main components, and these apply to *any* negotiation. When you commit the four steps on our checklist to memory and utilize these three sections in our log, negotiations become more manageable.

Unless we're coaching only one person, we prefer to debrief team members individually. Depending on their role, we find each player's perspectives differ. This is a good thing. In either case, this offers a broad summary of the deal while also giving us the chance to know our clients.

You'll find the same holds true in a leadership negotiation. The better you know your players and their views on unsettled agreements, the more effective you'll be when it comes time to aligning your team. Unique backgrounds, expertise, and experiences provide a leader with a broader view of the negotiation. Each will have a different view when you ask, "Tell me where you're involved in this potential deal, and where do you think it stands?"

Our coaching goal for the debrief is consistent. We want our clients to shift focus from their own assumptions, expectations, and emotions to the world of their opponent. What have they learned? How our client interprets the other side's actions and behaviors is the important part of the discussion. From the start of the negotiation to the conclusion, we want to understand and keep track of everything our clients have captured.

If you have the chance, ask someone at work to describe a negotiation in which they've recently been involved. They'll probably start by sharing their personal experiences. You'll get an entirely different picture if you ask, "What did you observe from the other side?" Dig deeper and ask questions like, "How did your opponent view the agreement? What did the other side have invested in the deal? What influenced their decision to sign the agreement?" The answers your coworker provides can be used for information when you're building a log.

THREE COMPONENTS OF A NEGOTIATION LOG: VISION, BUDGET, AND DECISION PROCESS

Paying close attention to these three areas is critical in *any* negotiated agreement. After each interaction, keep track of what's happening with your opponent. Here are example questions to ask yourself while building a log:

1. **Vision**: What does your opponent see? What are they trying to accomplish? What problems are they trying to solve? What opportunities will they have because of an agreement?
2. **Budget**: What has your opponent invested in the deal? How much time, energy, money, and emotion have they devoted or displayed?
3. **Decision process**: What choices has your opponent made? What's behind their verdict? How would you describe their decision-making process? Who should be included from their side of the table in future decisions?

Your log captures the decisions already made, the vision behind those and future decisions, and assesses the status of the pending agreement. You'll also discover new problems and the overall nature, tone, and emotions displayed for the negotiation event.

You'll find you can use the information compiled in the log to build your checklist for the next iteration. This rhythm of preparing, executing, and debriefing will keep you and your team grounded and focused from start to finish.

If you're in a position of leadership, ask yourself, "How many agreements am I involved with on any given day?" It might be more than you can count. I recently asked my replacement in Ohio, Brigadier General Dave Johnson, the same question. He said, "Agreements are everywhere, in all directions. The goal in most of our daily meetings is to reach or reinforce an agreement."

I hope this doesn't seem overwhelming. You can do this on a notepad. If you do, you'll start to develop the habit of applying our system. In the next chapter we'll focus on the behaviors of our system, which keeps you centered in your opponent's world. For now, let's focus on examples of each of the three components.

VISION

Vision is the first step in our negotiation log. Try to imagine the advantage you would have during a business negotiation if you could see the proposed agreement through the eyes of your opponent. This concept of "your opponent's vision" is critical. Hopefully you'll find my recent leadership experience helpful in any negotiation you want to present to the vision of your opposition.

Looking back over the past five years in command, I've had many opportunities to address large groups of airmen. Luckily, I've been surrounded by other talented leaders who've provided me with constructive feedback. During my first event addressing a few hundred of our senior leaders in Ohio, days after being announced the new assistant adjutant general, I made a mistake. I presented my strategic vision before understanding how my teammates viewed the big picture.

I was overwhelmed and compelled to let everyone know where I stood on many issues and priorities. Although I had a sense of urgency to make numerous changes, I didn't take the time to build my teammates' vision on why they were necessary. A good rule of thumb when you're seeking any agreement is to take your time before making any presentation. Uncover your opponent's vision first. I remember my father saying, "The best presentation you'll give is the one the other party doesn't see. If you're in their world, you can present to what you've uncovered, not what you assume is important to them."

My intentions were good, and luckily I came across to the team unscripted and genuine. Although my staff informed me most of the crowd provided good feedback during the remainder of the conference, the lack of interaction with the crowd disturbed me. My team at headquarters agreed with my concerns.

Shortly after this event, I began traveling across the state having town hall meetings. During these smaller and more intimate settings, I engaged more effectively by soliciting the thoughts and concerns of the airmen. This improved the interaction. Rather than starting the meeting by presenting my solutions to problems, I opened the discussion with Q&A. The success I normally experienced connecting with my teammates individually became more of a challenge in front of a group. Reflecting on those first few months in command, I failed to see the perspective of the larger group before sharing my strategic vision for the state.

I followed up with countless private meetings with modest-sized leadership teams at each unit. When I decided to treat each encounter like a negotiation, my perspective changed. I started seeing their world more clearly. These one-on-one connections worked. Using the structure of our negotiation system, even during difficult discussions regarding job performance or disciplinary action, kept me relaxed and focused on the vision of my teammates. Instead of presenting my view on an issue up front, helping them see the problem from their point of view made the solution *their* idea.

Then it hit me: The size of the group didn't matter. These are simply negotiations with more people in the room.

During our annual leadership conference in February 2021, I had the chance to put this to the test. After months of smaller meetings and virtual events, our entire team met in person. Hundreds of military leaders in the Ohio National Guard gathered for three days. During the first day, the agenda included military briefings, speakers, and an overview of the previous year's challenges and accomplishments. For the morning of the second day, we blocked out four hours for private sessions with the air and army leadership teams. Normally we limited the audience to the senior leaders only. This year I wanted maximum capacity, including younger airmen. I wanted their perspective since they were closer to many of our problems.

My executive officer, Major Britney Hensley, met me in the lobby and seemed tense. When I asked her what troubled her, she replied, "Sir, you're getting ready to face a tough crowd." She explained that the previous day's feedback was not good. The team felt like they were being talked at and didn't appreciate an entire day of being in receive mode. With the event canceled in previous years due to COVID-19, she stressed, "Today is important. They need an opportunity to talk. They must feel engaged."

My state command chief and I had gotten used to speaking to our units together, and we considered this day an important opportunity to address challenges. In addition to numerous operational deployments, our recruiting and retention numbers were bad. The units and their leadership teams were fatigued from dealing with COVID-19, and the National Guard's unprecedented response to the pandemic pushed our people to the breaking point.

When Chief Master Sergeant Heidi Bunker approached me just prior to the start of our meeting, I let her know we were going to spend all our time, if necessary, listening to our folks. Instead of focusing on our agenda for numerous strategic challenges, and instead of executing the mental checklist we created in preparation for this group, we both agreed to listen. We sincerely wanted to hear from everyone. We wanted their vision before we made any attempt to gain agreement on many decisions.

Walking into the crowded room, I put the first problem on the table for discussion. I said,

> This is our opportunity to share our vision of
> what we're all facing in the future. I don't want

the "rank" in the room interfering. The chief and I hope you're comfortable sharing your thoughts. The agenda for our discussion is up to you. If we run out of time, we will continue to follow up with all of you until you are heard. Let's start with the challenges you see in the field. If you think we're missing something at state headquarters, this is the time to bring it up. You can tell us no to any of our policies holding you back from accomplishing your missions. How can we help you? What's on your mind?

We quickly kicked off a three-hour negotiation. The chief and I stayed focused in their world, especially when they became emotional talking through tough issues. What may have seemed like a chaotic mess to a bystander started the process for solidifying enduring agreements. Creating a safe environment for our leaders to push back and say no led to a healthy debate. Many commanders had differing opinions, and younger airmen joined in without hesitation. Although many expressed disagreements at first, in the end the majority aligned to a collective vision. The chief and I were able to reach decisions with our team's full support.

Based on the after-action survey for the conference, most said, "This is the best commanders conference I've attended, and I appreciated being heard." They trusted their perspective mattered to the chief and me. Documenting everything discussed, we captured the vision, budget (in this case everyone's emotional commitment), and decision process of the collective group. Changes to policy and strategic direction were embraced by our team. They were all part of the process, and they were emotionally invested in the agreement.

BUDGET

The second step in the negotiation log is budget. This is determined by evaluating how much time, energy, money, and emotion your counterpart has invested in the negotiation. The more someone's committed leading up to a verdict, especially emotionally, the more difficult it becomes to walk away from the agreement. Let's look at a typical sales situation to illustrate this concept.

We've all afforded a salesperson a few minutes of our *time* to present their product. If we're interested, we may decide to review literature, or even sit through a lengthy presentation. Now we've invested time and *energy*. Assuming the price is something we can afford, or if we go a step further by putting down a deposit, our budget has grown to include *money*. Time, energy, and money are all important. Once the customer starts to visualize the impact of the product or service, and how they can solve problems by buying the product, their *emotional commitment* to the decision increases.

During a recent coaching session with sales associates from one of the largest car dealerships in the country, we spent an hour on the concept of budget. One of our top sales coaches, Mike Lewandowski, led the call. Mike is a sales professional with over twenty-five years of experience. He started working with the Camp System in 2011. He recruited, trained, and led his teams in negotiations with many of the most formidable procurement departments within the world's premier automotive manufactures. Mike grew one company's service business from eight million dollars to forty million dollars per year with our system.

Here's what Mike had to say:

> Once emotions enter the equation, the decisions for everyone involved become more difficult. When you see your client start to get excited about a car, it's important for you to stay calm. I know it's hard to do, but you must control your expectations. The moment you start to show your need for a deal, you're in trouble. Your customer can sense your need and may hesitate. Stay relaxed, nurturing, and patient. Help them through their decision-making. This is a big purchase for them. Don't let your emotions get the best of you.

When the negotiation progresses, and the longer it lasts, budgets on both sides of the table can grow. Be cautious of your own budget. In business, openly displaying your emotions can reveal your need for the deal. If your need becomes exposed, be prepared for your counterpart to push for a compromise.

Another challenge with managing your personal budget in a deal is avoiding the sunk cost fallacy. Once you've put too much into an agreement, it can be hard for you to walk away. Try to recognize the point where your personal commitment to a negotiation interferes with good decision-making.[1]

DECISION PROCESS

Hopefully, you've addressed decision making, the third component of the negotiation log. Avoid the assumption you're negotiating with a qualified person who can decide. If you do, be prepared for a surprise. Even if your opponent tells you explicitly, "I'm the decision maker," it could be more complicated than you expect.

Unless you have firsthand knowledge of the decision process, you might subject yourself to wasted time, increased energy, unnecessary expenses, and emotional frustration. If you assume how decisions are made in the deal, your own budget will increase. In addition to the questions, I suggested previously, ask yourself:

1. What have I learned of the opposition's decision process?
2. Who must say yes, or who can say no and block the deal?
3. Who influences the decision-makers?
4. When do the additional decision-makers surface, and how can I gather their vision?

In a recent sales negotiation, we were engaged with a large energy provider in Europe. The company's global sales teams were having trouble meeting earnings expectations. Their vice president of global sales reached out to us looking for help. He shared his teams were leaving money on the table due to disjointed negotiations. Too many contracts faced renewal, and the disparity in agreed pricing between his teams needed immediate attention.

They lacked consistency with their team's performance. Individual talent determined the success of the sales teams. With over two dozen sales leads functioning autonomously, and a high level of attrition, the VP found himself unable to oversee and lead his team effectively. The company did not provide consistent training or a systematic approach for managing their larger agreements.

We put together a mission and purpose for the VP:

> By adapting a systematic approach and coaching to their sales negotiations, each sales leader would gain control of their preparation, clearly identifying roles and responsibilities for each team member. This would ensure optimized pricing and delivery terms for their deals. Unnecessary compromise would be avoided, and a consistent pricing strategy could stabilize each market segment.

Unless we implemented a long-term training program, followed by direct coaching support on critical sales negotiations, we knew we'd be unable to execute our M&P. Without a major commitment to change, their sales would continue to suffer. Although we gathered a clear picture of their challenges, which is the decision we wanted for the first call, we knew what happened next required a detailed look into the potential scope of training and coaching.

Before our team at Camp executed the next call, we built a script asking the following questions:

- What's at stake for your company financially?
- How much risk are you facing with your team's performance?
- What would success look like?
- How much are you leaving on the table with these deals?
- What is your leadership willing to budget for training and coaching to secure higher margins?
- Help us understand how decisions are reached within your company. Who should we include from your senior leadership on the next call?

Reviewing our notes and compiling a summary for our negotiation log, we identified problems in all three sections. The VP didn't have a realistic vision of solving his sales teams' challenges. He hoped a two-day training event would be enough. Don't get me wrong, training can be valuable. His case warranted coaching. I remember thinking, *He wants us to sell him a Band-Aid when he really needs to call a doctor.*

Under pressure from his C-level leadership to increase profits, his emotional budget continued to grow. Unfortunately, he didn't have the money for anything beyond a training workshop. Even though coaching his teams on important deals would yield a significant return on investment, he couldn't get access to more resources.

We discovered another issue with his decision: He alone couldn't make the call. We were required to submit a competing bid with the CFO and board approving the cost for training and coaching.

The budget on our side was low at this point. Although we invested time for research and preparing for this negotiation and spent an hour on a call, we had no money and little emotion invested in our decision. While we could have submitted a bid for a two-day workshop at their headquarters in Europe, we elected to stick to our mission and purpose. We didn't want to compromise on our delivery for the sake of revenue. We decided not to provide a partial solution. We knew this was not going to solve his problem.

In this example, all three sections of the log—vision, budget, and decision process—revealed challenges preventing an agreement. Their VP elected to bring in another training program. Based on the preliminary results of a previous quarter, the VP recently circled back to Camp, hoping to reengage.

Vision, budget, and decision process are *required* in our system. Whether you're in a one-on-one agreement with a peer, boss, or subordinate, negotiating with a large group of teammates, or involved with a complex business deal, these three areas are required. Simply remembering these three items gives you emotional control and focus. These can also help you plan for the next interaction.

Your focal point during negotiation should be your opponent's vision. You should seek to help people capitalize on opportunities and solve problems. Using a system will bring you closer to a deal. You'll start building their budget when they become more invested in the decision, especially your opponent's emotional commitment. Unfortunately, simply *telling* your opponent doesn't mean they'll realize what you're suggesting can help. The key to helping anyone connect emotionally is asking questions and listening. This is where you'll uncover what really matters.

Remember, the decision process for any agreement is impeded by emotions. In the next chapter we'll examine my most challenging years in leadership. Here we'll move beyond the structure of a checklist and log and identify the behaviors of the Camp System. You'll see how your posture and communication can make the difference during a long and difficult leadership negotiation.

CHAPTER 11

YOUR BEHAVIORS— POSTURE AND COMMUNICATION

From earlier in the book, you might recall me saying you can only control two aspects of any negotiation, your activity and behavior. I know we've spent a lot of time examining the importance of systematic preparation and debriefing. The benefits of developing a checklist and analyzing each step can help you stay calm and focused. Like any competitive sport, no amount of strategy and practice guarantees yours or your teams' performance. The habit of preparation alone gives you an emotional edge. Knowing you've done everything you could to prepare allows you to execute your game plan and react to your competitor with confidence. How you behave during the game is critical. Your posture throughout a deal leads to trust, and how you communicate dictates your ability to remain centered in your opponent's world.

From my personal experiences, the same behaviors that make you a more effective negotiator will also help you become a better leader. Regardless of your personality or strengths and weaknesses, be yourself when you negotiate or lead people. Please keep in mind, I'm not suggesting radical changes in the way you operate. Instead, I'm hopeful you'll see how making small behavioral changes can result in lasting agreements.

BE AWARE OF YOUR STRENGTHS AND WEAKNESSES

The best leadership advice I've received came from my predecessor, Brigadier General Greg Schnulo. Before stepping into my new role, he said, "Be true to who you are and what you stand for. You're the right person at the right time. Have confidence in your abilities, Jim, and be yourself." Greg knew me well. He understood my strengths and weaknesses. Serving together for over twenty years, we would often discuss my natural intensity. He has a natural way of helping people see how others perceive them. I've taken this to heart. I continue to work on controlling my behavior even today, and I'm grateful for his patience and encouragement during my military career.

Over the years, I've given similar advice trying to help young leaders and negotiation clients develop more self-awareness. I've emphasized the importance of staying true to who you are while also avoiding complacency. Managing your behavior is an ongoing challenge. Successful leadership and negotiation require humility and the willingness to learn from your mistakes. Despite your best intentions, obsessing over results during the heat of a deal can derail your intended behavior.

I've been there many times myself, especially early in my career. When I sensed things not going my way, my natural intensity would surface in the form of frustration. Instead of executing my checklist, I'd start talking too much, trying to convince others to lean in my direction. For people who know me well, my facial expressions or tone in my voice signaled my agitation. Like everyone else reading this, my own behavior is still a work in progress. Becoming a more effective negotiator doesn't necessitate changing your natural tendencies. Be aware of them. When you sense you're losing control, focus on your mission and purpose and how your agreement can benefit those you're negotiating with.

I believe whole heartedly in the cliché, "Your greatest strength can become your greatest weakness." If you're compassionate and care for your people, you'll build trust and loyalty with your team. If you're competitive and approach challenges with intensity, you'll probably have a better chance of overcoming adversity. Those who can inspire others as charismatic speakers create an atmosphere of optimism. Intelligent individuals with the ability to solve complex problems build confidence in those they work with.

Here's the problem with the strengths I've mentioned. If you're too smart and unable to embrace feedback from your team, your solutions to problems may not be optimal. Charisma will only get you to a certain point when you *need* to talk and dominate the conversation. Competitiveness and intensity can get the best of you. Instead of listening and staying patient, you might become self-focused and pushy. Compassion can lead to inaction or indecision, especially when it comes to making hard decisions regarding your teammates.

We can make the same analogies in the negotiation arena. The way you naturally behave might make you successful on one deal and can lead to failure on the next. When it comes to reaching agreements, simply relying on what's gotten you this far is not enough. We all can improve.

In our system we've identified consistent behaviors giving you the best chance for success. The good news is, we believe these are time-tested and apply to any deal. We don't believe in applying leverage, tricks, or high-pressure tactics. Those types of behaviors will not build trust and gain the respect of your opponent. Perhaps you've been on the receiving end of someone trying to manipulate your emotions during a negotiation.

YOUR POSTURE-NURTURING VERSUS APPLYING PRESSURE

The ability to consistently maintain a nurturing and respectful posture is the most important and fundamental behavior in our system. Nurturing behavior helps others comfortably hear what you're saying and share what they see. Treating people with respect lowers their emotions and helps them make effective decisions.[1]

How you communicate with your opponent must be seen through this lens. The most nurturing way to build vision and stay centered in your opponent's world is to ask good questions with this demeanor in mind. The best decisions are made with emotions in a neutral position. If you're calm and relaxed, your opponent will mirror your behavior. What happens to your emotions when you're dealing with someone who's calm and respectful? The more you can remain nurturing and respectful, the more people will trust you and their decisions.

The moment you allow your emotions to swing too far positive or negative, you run the risk of adversely impacting their decision-making process. Excitement can create hesitation on the other side. If you're fighting too hard to convince someone to agree, they will sense your need for the deal. Either response triggers skepticism and the fear of making a bad decision.

We've all been subjected to pressure and persuasion. People who have perceived power and leverage may try to force you into an agreement. You've probably heard the saying, "Take it or leave it," or, "There will be consequences if you say no." Even if you're not in a leadership position, we've all watched leaders make the mistake of using fear and intimidation to force decisions. In the past, when you made a significant purchase, chances are you've been subject to the salesperson employing high pressure closing techniques. Using aggressive measures forcing decisions is not respectful and nurturing behavior. From your experience, how effective are leaders when they use power and leverage against their teams? Leaders pushing too hard can damage relationships and trust. Agreements made under stress can collapse over time.

For those with business negotiation experience, you've probably encountered tricks and tactics used to push you into compromising. We see this often with our coaching clients. They often hear firm statements like, "What you're asking for is a non-starter," "You better sharpen your pencil," "I can't take this to my leadership," or, "You're way more expensive than your competition." These statements are designed to impact your emotions and create the fear of losing a deal. What's really behind the tricks and tactics at the negotiation table? From a negotiation coaching perspective, this type of behavior is weak and ineffective. When we're coaching, we help our clients realize the one pushing the hardest for a decision in a deal is the most vulnerable.

Keep in mind applying pressure is taking away someone's comfort in saying no. This is why the most nurturing and respectful thing you can do in any negotiation is give your counterpart the ability to veto. Out of mutual respect, your opposition will sense an obligation to share their reasons for rejecting. Once they begin to let you in, keeping the same posture gives you the chance to ask the right questions.

NURTURING COMMUNICATION—ASKING THE RIGHT QUESTIONS

If you can improve your ability to ask better questions, your leadership and negotiation success will improve dramatically.

Questions can build vision and help you understand what your opponent sees. With the proper wording and method of delivery, you can uncover important information without making someone uneasy. If you prepare good questions before your engagement, you'll be shocked at what you discover. The biggest mistake you can make asking any question is pushing for a decision too soon.

According to my brother, Todd,

> The most important thing our clients can do to gain an edge is script out a few questions that can build and uncover vision. Interrogative-led or open-ended questions help you understand what someone is thinking. The problem is that many people have developed the habit pattern of asking verb-led questions. I know it seems subtle, but asking questions that begin with what, how, when, where, and sometimes why are always more effective than questions beginning with can you, will you, is, are you, or do you. Verb-led questions force a decision.

We don't gather vision when we hear yes, no, or maybe, and our opponent may not be ready to decide. Unless you're trying to confirm something you already know to be true, you'll learn more by asking an interrogative. This behavioral habit alone will make a huge difference in your career.

Hopefully you've noticed throughout this entire book, I've asked many interrogative-led questions to help you see and discover key aspects of our system. To illustrate the magnitude of this behavior, let's look at the difference this made with one of our recent clients. If you've spent time in a car dealership you may have been subject to high pressure sales tactics. Despite research suggesting high pressure doesn't work on consumers, a trend still lingers in the car business of applying pressure on customers making difficult decisions.[2]

Recently, a large car dealership reached out to us for sales negotiation coaching. Working with sales teams is normal; however, this would be our first opportunity to coach in the retail automobile sector. Their leadership team wanted to reinforce a low-pressure car buying atmosphere and integrate our system into the culture of their sales professionals. Coaching close to a hundred professionals, we noticed most were rooted in the habit of asking verb-led questions. Although their questions were intended to help the salesperson understand the needs of their customers, they were missing the mark. While the individual questions themselves wouldn't be considered "high-pressure," they were inadvertently forcing the buyer to make too many incremental decisions. Small changes in the way they asked questions made a big difference.

For example, instead of asking, "Are you looking for a new or used vehicle?" they learned more by asking, "What type of vehicles are you considering?" and, "What concerns do you have in choosing a vehicle?" or, "How do you intend to use the vehicle?" With these new questions, they started connecting with their customers' vision, budget, and decision process. They learned more after only a few interrogative-led questions than they expected. This saved time and kept the sales team focused on their prospects' world.

Because the sales staff openly gave their customers the right to say no, which eased the normal pressures of buying a car, they sold more vehicles. At the end of the negotiation, and with a better picture of what their clients were trying to accomplish, they no longer needed to close the deal. Before starting the eight-week coaching program, they would normally try to close the deal by asking, "Are you ready to leave here today in this car?" The questions after shifted to, "Where are we at this point, what other concerns do you have, or what else can we provide to help you with your decision today?"

This new nurturing and respectful approach to communicating with their customers resulted in more sales and a better car buying experience for the customer.

Their entire team was aligned to our system and speaking the same negotiation language.

LEADERSHIP NEGOTIATION—BEHAVIOR CASE STUDY

While preparing to retire from the military, I had many candid conversations with my fellow leaders discussing the challenges we faced over the past few years. They all related to me when I said, "I've learned more in the past few years of my career than I did in my first thirty."

Beginning in March of 2019, leadership across the entire National Guard faced problems beyond the scope of their training and imagination. Starting with the global shutdown due to the pandemic, followed by historic domestic responses in support of state governors, our leaders were dealing with too much. To make matters worse, the continuous oversea deployments and the military's COVID-19 vaccine mandate made it more difficult than usual to keep servicemembers in uniform. Unfortunately, the military has suffered high numbers of personnel separations. Many separated prematurely, leaving a lifetime of benefits and pensions on the table.

The pressures of leadership are inherently difficult. With numerous problems emerging during a crisis, emotions can overcome any leader's behavior. Reflecting on the challenges of COVID-19, I collaborated more frequently with my trusted teammates. With little guidance from higher-ups in headquarters, we had to figure out how to safely operate our units without losing sight of our duty to execute our missions. For our commanders, the pressures of keeping our bases functioning and combat ready were significant. I'm the one ultimately held accountable for personnel and mission readiness, and my commanders turned to me to answer hard questions: "How are we supposed to safely fly aircraft and deploy our forces during a pandemic?" "Our people aren't doing well in isolation. How do we keep them engaged?"

I suppose our situation in the Ohio National Guard during COVID-19 was like a company facing bankruptcy. Imagine a CEO trying to keep the lights on, running out of capital, and losing talented people once they discovered the company might go under. The number of internal daily agreements within our units, staff, other state agencies, and headquarters were unprecedented. Senior leaders quickly discovered *they* didn't necessarily have the best solutions. Luckily their smaller teams were closer to the problems and offered innovative solutions. We couldn't simply give orders; we had to nurture solutions by listening to our teams' ideas.

Once each unit developed a plan to safely operate, we faced an even bigger problem: the federal vaccine mandate. What at first seemed like a simple mitigation to the disease turned into a nightmare. The question on our leader's minds became, "How do we comply with the vaccine mandate when our people were threatening to quit over the shot?" We all knew this could be catastrophic for the future of our units.

Members of my team pointed out, "This shouldn't be up for debate. Our folks need to agree to the shot, or face being kicked out." They were correct. Taking the shot is a lawful order, and I would be the one responsible for signing discharge orders when they refused. I decided to take a different approach. We had an opportunity to negotiate with our airmen.

In my mind, we had nothing to gain by starting the negotiations with harsh demands. The airmen already knew the stakes were high. Because this is an emotional and politically charged decision for our folks, our leaders needed to keep a nurturing and respectful posture. We had to start the conversations by acknowledging the airmen's option to refuse. Nurturing didn't mean we could offer them a compromise. Instead, we needed to ask questions and listen. We wanted to get into their world and understand their vision.

Don't get me wrong. I didn't want to give the impression our airmen would be let off the hook. My agenda included their awareness of timelines and consequences for refusing the vaccine. At times in any negotiation, you can't save your opponent from making a difficult decision. I also wanted our leadership to display empathy for their hard decision. I knew seeking a choice early could help the airmen move past their emotions and enable them to start intellectually justifying their decision. Remember, decisions can be changed. A "no" doesn't mean the negotiation is over.

A leader's control of the narrative is important during a crisis. Facing hard decisions doesn't get better over time. In the absence of direct guidance, your teammates will fill the void with rumors and conjecture. Delaying the negotiation would only exacerbate their emotions, making the situation worse. The same holds true in a business negotiation. If you ignore or delay communicating problems, you'll lose trust and credibility with your opposition.

To preserve our airmen's trust, Chief Heidi Bunker and I sensed an urgency to connect with our airmen in person. Logistically this was difficult, and we knew this was not the time to shoot a video or send out a long-winded email. We connected with our command teams by organizing town hall discussions across the state. Instead of trying to negotiate in mass, we wanted dozens of small group opportunities. With too large of an audience, we would miss out on the chance to engage individually. With discharge actions only ninety days away, we needed to move quickly. We developed our mission and purpose and at the start of each meeting, affording the opportunity of our airmen to say no. We knew this would lower their emotions and uncover what's influencing their decisions.

In each meeting, we initiated with a brief problem statement, followed with an interrogative-led (or open-ended) question. For example, based on my other position as the National Guard advising the commander of US Transportation Command, I shared the challenges of global mobility during the pandemic. I said, "We have a huge challenge today. Logistically we cannot transition through many of our ports due to the vaccine requirements of our allies and partners." In a calm and nurturing manner, I asked the question, "What will it look like if we're called to action? Given the health concerns and stress on the military medical infrastructure, how can we protect our teammates from getting sick when we deploy?"

Instead of telling the airmen all the facts and data supporting the vaccine mandate, we asked questions helping them *see* the problems. We also encouraged our folks to share their personal objections to taking the vaccine. Because they were responding from their point of view and not simply being "talked to," they let their guard down, and we listened.

Hearing why they wanted to refuse the shot surprised us. Many feared what they read on various social media outlets. Others aligned their decisions to political affiliation. One gentleman informed us his wife threatened to not have children if he took the shot. The more they voiced their concerns, the more their emotions surfaced. I remember Chief Bunker telling me, "This is a good thing, boss. Let them talk to you. They need us to listen."

When a young airmen attacked me verbally for pushing this mandate in Ohio, I said, "I don't blame you for being upset. I know this is hard for many of you. What would you have me do in this scenario? Unfortunately, we must follow military guidelines." When you're attacked verbally, human nature is to plant your feet and fight for your position. In any negotiation, this is not effective. A confrontation will only elicit an emotional response. In coaching we call this a "strip-line and reverse." When emotions swing too far negative, stay nurturing and allow your opponent to attack. After using a supportive statement and empathizing with their emotions, we teach our clients to *reverse* the harsh statement or question by asking another interrogative-led question.

Even if you're getting angry or frustrated, stay calm. By not taking their attack personally and allowing them to save face, you're helping them process their emotions. This keeps your opponent feeling okay and safe. When others in the room witnessed my calm reaction to what might have appeared borderline disrespectful, the level of trust in the room improved.

Although the chief and I were connecting well with our teammates, their initial decisions were concerning. Many airmen initially told their supervisors no to the vaccine. At first glance, our preliminary data suggested Ohio was leading the nation in potential discharges. When the first deadline for taking the shot passed, our commanders remained steadfast and implemented disciplinary action. Though a few of the airmen reversed their decision when they were facing a reprimand, we suspected many would hold out until the last minute. When the negotiation became increasingly uncomfortable with the final deadline approaching, we encouraged our leaders to remain calm. We couldn't force an agreement. If someone is willing to leave the military over the shot, we still wanted to respect their final decision.

We scheduled our final town hall with our F-16 maintenance group in Toledo, Ohio. The unit recently returned from deployments in Eastern Europe and Afghanistan, and the time for administering the shot was running out. The 180th Fighter Wing is an extremely tight unit with a strong lean-forward attitude. They have fighter jets on alert twenty-four seven and protect the airspace for half of the nation's population from another 9/11 event. Going into the hangar, the chief and I sensed a strong anti-vax sentiment. With my patience wearing thin, I had to paint a clear picture of what would happen next. We both were fatigued after dozens of engagements. With the deadline approaching, we gravitated to the groups with the highest number of noes. We hoped to reverse their decisions.

I mentioned previously you cannot save your opponent from tough decisions. We didn't have another shot negotiating with this group. Thankfully, Chief Heidi Bunker pulled me aside prior to the talk. She sensed my impatience and encouraged me to stick with our original approach. I took her advice. I started the meeting in a relaxed manner and listened respectfully. Nearing the end of our meeting, my natural intensity surfaced. With time running out, and no reason to hold back, I took a few deep breaths and paused for a moment to collect my thoughts. I couldn't end the negotiation without helping them *see* the impacts and ramifications of their decisions. In this case, I wanted an answer from everyone.

I remember saying, "Here's what's going to happen next. Russia might decide to shoot the Slovakian gap, and they could make an aggressive move in Eastern Europe. When we get the initial notification to prepare to deploy, this unit will have roughly three days to get out of the door to go execute our nation's will. While you're out-processing and saying goodbye to your families, you'll also be making sure your powers of attorney, wills, and medical items are squared away. If you're telling us you're going to step out of the medical processing line, refuse the shot, and not deploy with your brothers and sisters in arms, we want to know your decision today. We are out of time. We will respectfully initiate the discharge process. If you're going to leave, if you're going to say no, do it today. If you're leaving, tell us today. We need to start recruiting and training your replacements. Too much is riding on this unit's ability to project combat air power."

At the end of the vaccine mandate, Toledo's 180th Fighter Wing had only a few vaccine refusals. The leadership at the 180th and other units in Ohio displayed patience throughout the ordeal. Respecting the airmen's decision up until the last minute made the difference, especially in Toledo. Although leading up to the final days, one could have made the argument we pushed people to a no. In the end, however, when it came time to take the shot or face an immediate discharge, the vision of "what happens next" became too painful. The vast majority of our initial noes took the vaccine. Even in business, when the other side of the table believes you're willing to end a deal, this alone can make all the difference.

Despite the military's losses to the vaccine and continuing recruiting challenges, the Ohio Air Guard is still at the top of the nation in retention and recruiting. According to Ohio's Assistant Adjutant General for Air, Brigadier General David Johnson, "The Ohio Air Guard is ranked one of the highest in the country for recruiting and retention. We're consistently manned above our authorized end-strength and can handle any mission the Air Force sends our way."

Rely on your trusted teammates for support. I've always said, "Leadership is a team sport." Hopefully you agree the same thing can be said of the negotiation arena. Controlling your own behavior is hard, and it takes a trusted team's support to help you change. This is perhaps the most important agreement you'll make with your closest teammates: "Keep me honest and tell me what I need to hear and exactly when I need to hear it." I'm thankful for people like Chief Heidi Bunker for pulling me aside and telling me to take a break and regroup.

If a leader cares deeply for his or her people and believes in the mission of the organization, the internal negotiation can become fatiguing. Jim Sr. used to say, "The most dangerous negotiations you'll find yourself in are the ones you don't realize you're in and those you're not prepared for." In hindsight, I can remember many times in my career where I should have delayed or postponed difficult leadership negotiations. If you find yourself unable to control your emotions, or your natural strengths begin to override your intended posture and ability to effectively communicate, take a step back.

Even when you don't have the luxury of time, behave in a nurturing and respectful manner. The best way to gain respect is to offer it to those you're negotiating with.[3] If you find yourself dealing with teammates who seem highly emotional, or unwilling to move in your direction, don't become discouraged. Keep in mind, they'll remember everything you say and how you say it.

CONCLUSION

My early plan for my career didn't include thirty-four years in the military. Up until 9/11, I didn't see myself making it to twenty. I doubt I'm the only one with an unpredicted path in life. In retrospect, walking away from the family business to serve full-time in the military helped me in ways I didn't foresee. Although it seemed like I hit the pause button on my business career, leading people did not slow my growth in negotiation. I didn't realize military leadership is a continuous exercise in reaching and maintaining agreements. My two career paths complemented each other, and it took me years to figure it out. My success in leadership came from a system of negotiation, and my leadership journey has made me a better coach.

Writing this book has helped me appreciate my unique career opportunities. Reflecting on my past experiences helped me realize none of us can control the challenges coming our way. If you're a leader, you can't predict the deals you'll find yourself negotiating. We can't dictate our wins and losses, and we certainly don't have the ability to control the decision-making of others. We can, however, control our own decisions.

The desire for growth in leadership negotiation is *your* decision, one leading to more effective behaviors and resulting in lasting agreements. If you decide to apply a systematic approach to your important deals, you'll gain control over your emotions. If you're willing to embrace a "no" instead of fearing the word, and you're open to the idea that compromise is not always required to reach a deal, you're off to a great start.

Deciding to change your mindset in negotiation is hard. Having a good mindset in negotiation also necessitates your ability to let go of results. I know results are important; however, constantly focusing on results may lead to losing sight of what matters. To get what you want from any agreement, understand how your opponent makes decisions. Regardless of the deal you're trying to reach, your opponent's emotions impact their ability to decide. This is why we do what we can to lower emotions in a deal, including our own.

Enduring agreements necessitate trust, and respecting the decisions of others instantly builds it. Openly giving someone the right to say no puts people at ease. This opens a door to uncovering *their* vision. Taking the pressure off by allowing a person to reject also provides you the opportunity to find out what's holding them back from a "yes." Demonstrating your willingness to hear the word "no" reduces your perceived *need* for a deal and gives you a chance to see what's driving their decision.

By remembering the four reasons why people say no, you can determine what's holding them back. Do they lack the emotional *vision* of benefit? Maybe they don't see clearly enough how saying yes helps them. Is *data* available to support their decision? More information might be needed. Another possibility is they don't have the *authority* to decide. Perhaps they need to include others before agreeing. Finally, they could be telling you no to *bluff* and test you. They want to see how you react or see if you'll offer a compromise.

If you're leading a team and your own people express pushback, this is not a bad thing. You're already building trust by listening to their concerns. At least when you hear a "no" from your own people, you have a shot at getting to know them on a deeper level.

Even though leadership in any organization implies a degree of authority, achieving team cohesion and alignment is not a given. Connecting with your internal partners and getting to know them is important. When you're tempted to push hard for a solution you want them to support, remember your teammates reach tighter agreements when you take time to listen and learn. True buy-in takes patience. Even if your back is against the wall, leaders willing to slow down reach consensus sooner. If you don't get the answers you want, this doesn't mean the deal is coming to an end. Instead of pushing for the results you want, do the opposite. Ask good questions and help people share what they see. Remember, you want to focus on their world.

This leads us to the first step in your negotiation checklist. I acknowledge leaders may not have time to prepare for each iteration. When you do have the time, a quick checklist is extremely helpful in getting focused. Take a few minutes to craft a simple mission and purpose (M&P). This is our foundation for *any* negotiation event, internal or external. Don't confuse a negotiation purpose with the results you're looking for. In our system, a valid M&P must focus on the benefit of your opponent. The best way to develop one is asking yourself, "What am I trying to help them see and discover? How do they benefit with the proposed agreement I'm suggesting?" A good mission and purpose will guide your decision-making in any deal, especially when you encounter problems.

You'll rarely put together a deal without facing challenges. Potential problems holding you back from an agreement should be your second step. In this portion of the checklist, remember, you want to uncover and address problems early in the deal. I know this seems counterintuitive. You might feel tempted to move past issues, hoping nothing will surface. This is a mistake, especially in front of your team. A leader's willingness to take problems head-on builds trust. While you're prioritizing potential problems, tackle the biggest one first, and don't overlook emotional baggage. If you, or your opponent, bring emotional issues into the agreement, they can't be dismissed. When you ignore baggage, you run the risk of it surfacing later in the deal. When you fail to accomplish this step, problems can prevent you from getting the decisions you want.

Most agreements are a collection of decisions from both sides of the table. Decisions help the negotiation progress, indecision does not. This is why the third step in the checklist is important. Identify the decisions you want to make, and prepare for those you're seeking. Keep in mind the dangers of pushing too hard. When someone's not ready to decide, trying to force them can make you appear needy. Instead, set the agenda with your counterpart, giving them the ability to reject at any time. If they struggle, allow them to say no. You can prepare for this. Either way, you want *decisions*. Once you have them, you can focus on the final preparation section, which is reaching an agreement on what happens next.

This section can be fluid. If the other side is unable to decide, you get a hard "no" or a quick "yes," which seems too easy. Slow down and uncover the vision behind their decision. What happens next can be simple, like asking your opponent, "Where do we go from here?" Whatever you do, make sure the next steps are clear and mutually understood. Even if it appears you hit the end of the road, your desire to stay the course and keep negotiating is up to you. When you or your team is unsure of the next step, it might be a good time to regroup and examine what you learned from your recent call or meeting. Breaking down the event using the negotiation log is an effective structure for debriefing.

Whether you recently had a one-on-one conversation with a coworker or sat across from a big group at a conference table, the simplicity of the negotiation log is intentional. Everything you gathered and observed from your opposition can be organized into three areas. Capturing the vision, budget, and decision process of each person involved is ideal. Vision is simply your interpretation of what's important to the other side. If you stay focused in their world, and they comfortably share their position, you'll have plenty of information.

Remember, your opposition's budget is determined by the amount of time, energy, money, and emotion they've invested in the deal. With emotions having the most impact on someone's budget, their posture, what they said, and how they behaved are good indicators. The final section in the log is your knowledge of their decision process. In other words, how and when will they decide? Should you include others in the next meeting, or are you dealing with the right people?

Once you have a clear picture of what transpired, you can use this information to prepare the next checklist. Like I shared in the previous chapter, take the time to analyze your behaviors following the negotiation event. If you were unable to consistently remain nurturing and respectful, join the club. Controlling your behavior and communicating effectively is a work in progress for anyone who negotiates. Everyone will struggle with this from time to time.

Leadership negotiation is a human performance event. Like anything else you've tried to improve upon, getting better requires practice and repetition. In most cases, like most professional athletes, it warrants further study and coaching.

When I decided to write a book, I was transitioning from a full-time to part-time position in the military. Starting in 2023, I enjoyed the opportunity to jump back into negotiation coaching while still wearing the uniform. Sharing my thoughts on leadership negotiation with my clients grew my excitement on the subject. Many of the company leaders I worked with agreed their internal negotiations were the most difficult. This was the catalyst for me to dive into writing. Since starting this project nine months ago, I've spent an equal amount of time working with clients on leadership and business negotiations. Our system works with both. Although we protect our client confidentiality, I'm also thrilled to share the qualities I've seen coaching effective negotiators are the same qualities I've witnessed working with our best military leaders. Our system is effective with any form of negotiation. Learning a new system can be overwhelming, especially during your first exposure.

My brother, Todd, and I experienced this only two weeks ago. We conducted a private workshop with a large sales team. For nine hours we covered all aspects of our system. When we concluded, our clients admitted they were exhausted. The advice we gave them is the same I'd like to leave with you. If you're willing to take small steps with any of the concepts I've shared, you'll be pleased. In a low risk setting, watch how people behave when you give them the right to say no. If you haven't prepared for a negotiation using a structure, give it a shot. Be careful striving for win-win results and making unnecessary compromises. Look at your team and make the decision to get to know them better. The next time you sense your emotions taking over, step back and stay nurturing and respectful. Instead of asking a verb-led question, try to use an interrogative-led question.

I promise you, nothing here will get you in trouble with any agreement. If only a handful of people can benefit from this book, it will be well worth the effort. You can find me at Camp Negotiations. I welcome your feedback, even if you tell me no to what I've shared.

ACKNOWLEDGMENTS

Writing a book is a long journey. I can't imagine going through this without my wife Cynthia's support. Honey, I love you from the bottom of my heart.

I'm also grateful for the understanding and encouragement from my family. This process is consuming, and I know you've noticed my distraction. I hope you all know how much you've inspired me to put forth my best effort. I love you, and I'm looking forward to our future together. I'm truly blessed.

Thank you to the entire team at Camp Negotiations. Starting with my brother and business partner, Todd Camp: You're an amazing coach, and I look forward to growing this company together. The contributions from you and our coaching teammates, Dave DeSantis, Mark Glenewinkel, and Mike Lewandowski, are greatly appreciated.

I would also like to acknowledge the boldness and tenacity of our founder Jim Camp Sr. You paved the way for this company, Dad, and you'd be proud of our team.

Thank you to Major General John C. Harris Jr., the adjutant general in Ohio, for his support during my transition back into the business world.

To my military teammates, I'm honored to have served with all of you. Many of you encouraged me to write this, and I'm grateful for your inspiration and contributions.

CONTRIBUTORS

Major General Gary McCue, Brigadier General David Johnson, Brigadier General Clarence "Kenny" Maynus, Chief Master Sergeant (retired) Heidi Bunker, Chief Master Sergeant Troy Taylor, and Lieutenant Colonel Britney Hensley.

LEADERSHIP MENTORS

Lieutenant General Steven Nordhaus, Lieutenant General Michael Loh, Lieutenant General (retired) Scott Rice, Major General Duke Pirak, Major General Mark "Potsy" Webber, Major General John C. Harris Jr., Major General (retired) Deborah Ashenhurst, Major General (retired) Mark Bartman, Major General (retired) Harry "A.J." Feucht, Major General (retired) Steven Markovich, Major General (retired) Gene Hughes, Major General (retired) Laurie Farris, Major General (retired) Thomas Kennett, Major General (retired) Roger Williams, Brigadier General Mathew Woodruff, Brigadier General (retired) Gregory Schnulo, Brigadier General (retired) Todd Audet, Colonel (retired) Daniel Tack, Colonel (retired) Todd "T.K." Thomas, Colonel (retired) Jeffrey Lewis, Colonel (retired)

Eric "Zeb" Brown, Colonel (retired) James Jones, Colonel (retired) Douglas Pennington, Colonel (retired) Homer Rogers, Colonel (retired) Gregory Betts, Chief Master Sergeant (retired) John Ortiz, Chief Master Sergeant (retired) Thomas Jones, Chief Master Sergeant Edward Taylor, and Chief Master Sergeant (retired) Mark Dyer.

Finally, I would like to express my appreciation to the team at Manuscripts LLC. A special thanks to:

Carol McKibben, Cooper Anderson, Eric Koester, George Thorne, Gjorgji Pejkovski, Kristy Carter, Kristy Elam, Sherman Morrison, and Trisha Giramma.

This would not have been possible without your dedication and patience.

NOTES

Introduction

Jim Camp, *Start with No: The Negotiation Tools that the Pros Don't Want You to Know* (New York: Crown Currency, 2002).

Chapter 1: Negotiation and Leadership—A System Provides Emotional Control

Tejas Vemparala, "Solving the Mystery of Millennial and Gen Z Job Hoppers," *Business News Daily*, October 24, 2023, https://www.businessnewsdaily.com/7012-millennial-job-hopping.html.

Chapter 2: Negotiation and Leadership Mindset

Jennifer Smith, "Growth Mindset vs. Fixed Mindset: How What You Think Affects What You Achieve," *Mindset Health*, September 25, 2020, https://www.mindsethealth.com/matter/growth-vs-fixed-mindset.

Jim Camp, *Start with No: The Negotiation Tools that the Pros Don't Want You to Know* (New York: Crown Currency, 2002), 1–20.

Chapter 3: Decision Making—Don't Fear the "No"

Courtney Kube and Molly Boigon, "Every Branch of the Military Is Struggling to Make Its 2022 Recruiting Goals, Officials Say," *Military* (blog), *NBC News*, June 27, 2022, https://www.nbcnews.com/news/military/every-branch-us-military-struggling-meet-2022-recruiting-goals-officia-rcna35078.

Jim Camp, *Start with No: The Negotiation Tools that the Pros Don't Want You to Know* (New York: Crown Currency, 2002), 103.

Michael Schrage, "Daniel Kahneman: The Thought Leader Interview: The Nobel Prize-Winning Economist Parses the Roles of Emotion, Cognition, and Perception in the Understanding of Business Risk," *Strategy + Business a PWC publication*, Winter 2003, https://www.strategy-business.com/article/03409.

Chapter 4: Connection Is the First Negotiation

Dave Greene, "Stepping into a Key Leadership Position from the Outside," *Business-Leadership* (blog), *EO Johnson Business Technologies*, July 3, 2017, https://www.eojohnson.com/blog/business-leadership/egg-shells-red-carpet-stepping-key-leadership-position-outside.

Chapter 5: Checklist Step 1: Mission and Purpose— The Foundation for Negotiation

Jim Camp, *Start with No: The Negotiation Tools that the Pros Don't Want You to Know* (New York: Crown Currency, 2002), 91–94.

Chapter 6: Checklist Step 2: Problems and Baggage

Waverly Deutsch, "COVID-19 Is Changing Key Business Relationships," *CBR—Entrepreneurship* (blog), *Chicago Booth Review,* August 27, 2020, https://www.chicagobooth.edu/review/covid-19-changing-key-business-relationships.

Ray Riha, "What's Wrong with Our Leaders in the Workplace Today?" *American Business Magazine*, November 17, 2018, https://www.americanbusinessmag.com/2018/11/whats-wrong-with-our-leaders-in-the-workplace-today/.

Chapter 8: The Four Reasons People Say No—A Case Study

Jim Camp, *Start with No: The Negotiation Tools that the Pros Don't Want You to Know* (New York: Crown Currency, 2002), 159–160.

Chapter 9: Checklist Step 4: What Happens Next

Celine Wee, "'No' Seems to Be the Hardest Word: Why Getting a Yes/No Is Better than a 'Maybe'," *Medium*, December 23, 2022, https://celinewee.medium.com/no-seems-to-be-the-hardest-word-why-getting-a-yes-no-is-better-than-a-maybe-dbd5498e2483.

Jim Camp, *Start with No: The Negotiation Tools that the Pros Don't Want You to Know* (New York: Crown Currency, 2002), 67–68.

Amy Hudson, "Choose Your PT Test." *Air & Space Forces Magazine*, August 27, 2021, https://www.airandspaceforces.com/article/choose-your-pt-test/.

Chapter 10: Negotiation Log—What Just Happened

Emily Holland, "Unraveling Sunk Cost Fallacy Relationships," *ADR times* (blog), June 10, 2024, https://www.adrtimes.com/sunk-cost-fallacy-relationships/.

Chapter 11: Your Behaviors—Posture and Communication

Jim Camp, *Start with No: The Negotiation Tools that the Pros Don't Want You to Know* (New York: Crown Currency, 2002), 115–119.

Ronald A. Clark, "High Pressure Sales Tactics Are Outdated," *Springfield News-Leader*, February 21, 2015, https://www.news-leader.com/story/news/business/2015/02/21/high-pressure-sales-tactics-outdated/23810275/.

Shelby Deering, "14 Tiny Behavior Tweaks That Make People Respect You More, According to Psychologists," *Parade*, February 3, 2024, https://parade.com/living/how-to-gain-respect-according-to-psychologists.